HOW TO BE AN
Engineer

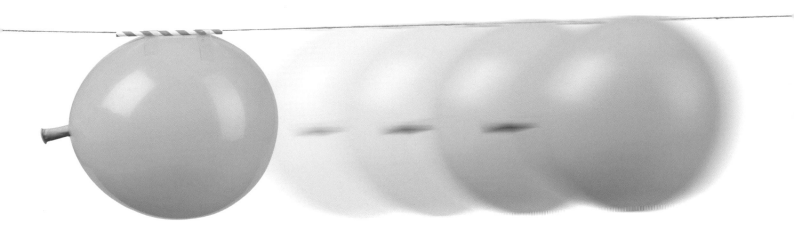

Consultant
Emily Hunt

Experts Benton Allen, Paige Earl, Trent Kelly
Consultant Emily Hunt

Senior editor Lizzie Davey
Senior art editor Jim Green
Additional editorial Jolyon Goddard,
Katy Lennon, Clare Lloyd, Claire Lister,
Meg Weal, Amina Youssef
Additional design Judy Caley, Emma Hobson,
Katie Knutton, Fiona Macdonald, Lucy Sims
US Senior editor Shannon Beatty
US Editor Liz Searcy
Jacket coordinator Francesca Young
Senior pre-production producer
Nikoleta Parasaki
Producer Basia Ossowska
Managing editor Laura Gilbert
Managing art editor Diane Peyton Jones
Creative director Helen Senior
Publishing director Sarah Larter

Some pages designed and edited
for DK by Dynamo Ltd.

First American Edition, 2018
Published in the United States by DK Publishing
345 Hudson Street, New York, New York 10014

Copyright © 2018 Dorling Kindersley Limited
DK, a Division of Penguin Random House LLC
18 19 20 21 22 10 9 8 7 6 5 4 3 2 1
001-307951-May/2018

A catalog record for this book is available from the Library of Congress.

ISBN: 978-1-4654-7027-0

DK books are available at special discounts when purchased in bulk
for sales promotions, premiums, fund-raising, or educational use. For
details, contact: DK Publishing Special Markets, 345 Hudson Street,
New York, New York 10014 SpecialSales@dk.com

Printed and bound in China.

A WORLD OF IDEAS:
SEE ALL THERE IS TO KNOW

www.dk.com

Contents

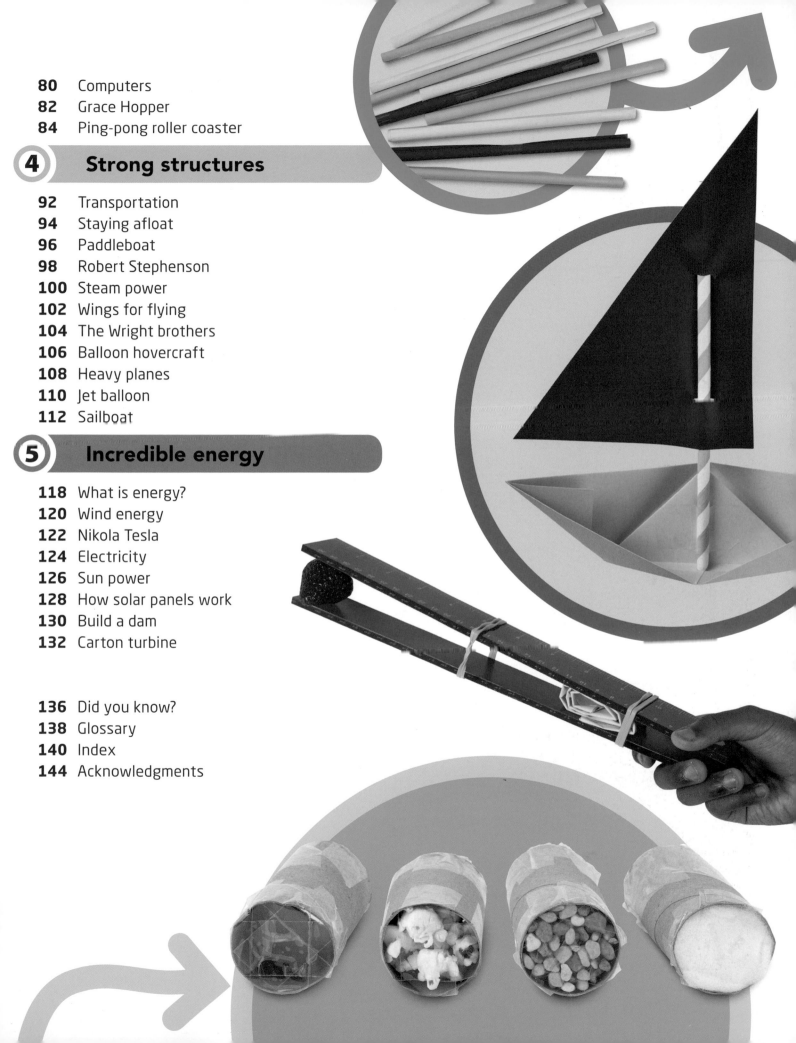

Do you like to explore how the things around you work? Do you want to create a new material? If so, you should be an engineer! Engineers use math and science to help people by creating solutions to problems.

If you want to be an engineer, it is important for you to learn how to solve problems and conduct experiments. Engineers and scientists both use experiments to test ideas. While scientists study how nature works, engineers create new things, like video games, better ways to grow food, and nanotechnology— technology so tiny you can see it using only special tools.

The first step in the engineering design process is to ask, What is the problem that needs solving? Then, engineers use their imaginations to come up with a plan based on things that they know or have found out by investigation. They then take their plan and create a design to solve the problem. The last step in the process is to do experiments to test the design, to improve it or make it better.

This book was written by our team of engineers to help you discover new ideas and learn more about the world around you. Come on, future engineers—let's get started!

Emily M. Hunt

How the book works

In *How to be an Engineer,* you will learn how to think and act like an engineer. The book is full of fun activities that can be done at home, as well as simple explanations and a look at some of the most famous engineers of all time.

Awesome activities

These pages feature engineering projects for you to try yourself. The results you get may not be the same as those in the book—but that's OK! If the results don't match up, try to figure out what you did differently, and then try it again.

What you will need for each experiment is listed at the top of the page.

The engineering behind each project is explained with the help of diagrams.

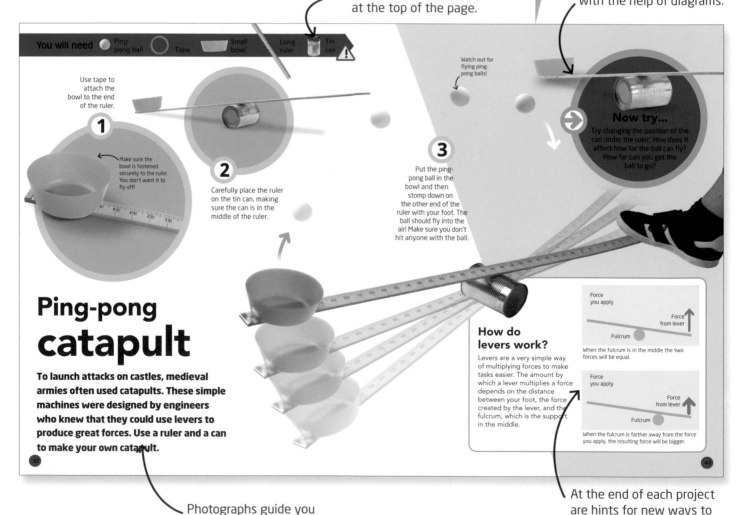

You will need — Ping-pong ball — Tape — Small bowl — Long ruler — Tin can ⚠

Use tape to attach the bowl to the end of the ruler.

1

Make sure the bowl is fastened securely to the ruler. You don't want it to fly off!

2

Carefully place the ruler on the tin can, making sure the can is in the middle of the ruler.

3

Put the ping-pong ball in the bowl and then stomp down on the other end of the ruler with your foot. The ball should fly into the air! Make sure you don't hit anyone with the ball.

Watch out for flying ping-pong balls!

Now try...
Try changing the position of the can under the ruler. How does it affect how far the ball can fly? How far can you get the ball to go?

Ping-pong catapult

To launch attacks on castles, medieval armies often used catapults. These simple machines were designed by engineers who knew that they could use levers to produce great forces. Use a ruler and a can to make your own catapult.

How do levers work?

Levers are a very simple way of multiplying forces to make tasks easier. The amount by which a lever multiplies a force depends on the distance between your foot, the force created by the lever, and the fulcrum, which is the support in the middle.

Force you apply — Force from lever — Fulcrum
When the fulcrum is in the middle the two forces will be equal.

Force you apply — Force from lever — Fulcrum
When the fulcrum is farther away from the force you apply, the resulting force will be bigger.

Photographs guide you through all of the steps.

At the end of each project are hints for new ways to test what you have learned.

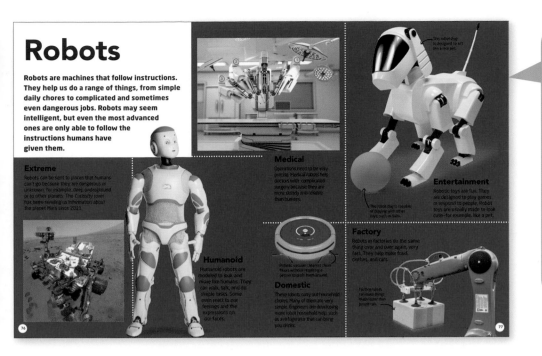

Robots

Robots are machines that follow instructions. They help us do a range of things, from simple daily chores to complicated and sometimes even dangerous jobs. Robots may seem intelligent, but even the most advanced ones are only able to follow the instructions humans have given them.

Cool engineering

The topics on these pages cover everything from materials and robots to transportation and energy. They will help you understand the activities in the book.

Leonardo da Vinci

Engineer and artist • Born 1452 • From Italy

When he wasn't painting masterpieces like the *Mona Lisa* or *The Last Supper*, Leonardo da Vinci was busy working as an engineer. In addition to developing catapults for the military, he filled his notebooks with amazing designs for flying machines, tanks, and even a robot!

"I know how... to make an infinite number of bridges."

Great engineers

The stories behind groundbreaking engineers are brought to life in these pages. Learn about their greatest discoveries, and find out what made them such brilliant engineers in the first place.

Safety first

All of the projects in this book should be done carefully. If you see this symbol at the top of a page, it means that you will need an adult to help you with the activity.

Be particularly careful when:

- you are using sharp objects, such as scissors, craft knives, thumbtacks, nails, or toothpicks

- you are using hot liquids

- you are using a hair dryer

- you are making things fly through the air

Getting ready

You can dive right into many of the projects in this book using items you have at home. There are also a few tools that may help with your engineering experiments. Thinking ahead is the first step to becoming an engineer.

Don't forget a pencil or pen so you can make notes!

If a project calls for cutting something, scissors are an essential tool.

What is an engineer?

Engineers use math and science to solve problems. They build some things so tiny you can't see them and others so big they can house thousands of people. Engineers work with materials, structures, machines, transportation, and energy. No matter what your skills are, there is an engineering role perfect for you!

Engineers come up with ways of doing things as well and as quickly as possible.

Use a ruler to measure length. It's important to be accurate.

Thinking like an engineer

Equipment can be useful, but being an engineer isn't always about having the right tools—it's about the way you think. This list of tips will help you think like an engineer.

1 Engineers always ask questions. Be curious, and find out as much information as you can before you start a project.

2 Engineers think about how things will look. Use your imagination to visualize exactly what you want to create.

3 Engineers are precise. Always double-check that you are using the right tools and the correct measurements.

4 Engineers are confident. You will succeed if you believe in yourself and your ideas.

5 Engineers regularly work in teams. You may prefer to work alone, but teamwork often produces some of the best results.

6 Engineers are problem solvers. Never give up. There is always a solution to the problem.

7 Engineers never stop. If you think an experiment or invention can be improved, go back to it, and see if you can make it better.

Waterproof

Metal

Flexible

Clay

Hard

Sand

Plastic

Strong

Wood

Stone

Amazing materials

Engineers have to think about what materials they use to build things. Materials have different properties. They can be soft, hard, flexible, or many other things. These properties make them useful for different purposes.

What are materials?

Every object that you can touch is made of something. Engineers call these somethings "materials." Materials have different qualities called properties—they can be strong, soft, stretchy, or solid. These qualities make them useful for different things.

This plastic is soft and can be made into different shapes.

Plastic

Plastic comes in all shapes and sizes. It can be hard or soft and can come in different colors. Plastic is used to make many things, from bags to boats!

Concrete

Concrete is made of a mixture of sand, gravel, cement, and water. It is liquid when freshly made, then it can be poured into a mold, where it sets, becoming hard and very strong.

Concrete blocks, like this one, can be used for building homes, bridges, office buildings, and many other things.

Wool can be spun into yarn.

Metal

Metals are strong and don't break easily. Metals let electricity move through them, and some are magnetic, which means they can pull other metals toward them. Metals are used for making structures inside buildings and for electric wires.

This metal wrench is strong. It can be used to tighten nuts and bolts.

Wood

Wood is a good material to use for kitchen utensils because it doesn't let heat travel through it.

Wood is a natural material, which means that it is not made by humans. Wood doesn't break easily and can last for a long time. It can be carved and fastened together to make furniture and other useful tools.

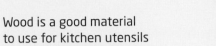

Wool

Wool is a natural material that grows on sheep. It is soft and warm, which makes it useful for making warm clothes and carpets.

Nanomaterials

Nanomaterials are made of particles so tiny that you can't see them with the naked eye—you have to use a super-strong microscope. Engineers work at this miniature scale to create materials that can do amazing things, such as reflect light.

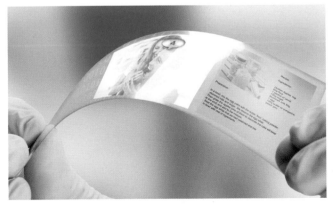

Wafer-thin computer This transparent piece of graphene is as thin as a piece of paper. It is made using nanotechnology and can display videos.

13

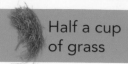
Making
mud bricks

Mixing different materials together can make them stronger, softer, or squishier. For making buildings, we need strong materials, such as bricks. They start off as soft materials but end up solid, strong, and hard.

Line the ice cube tray with plastic wrap. Spoon your mixture into each hole, and press it down into the holes.

2

The plastic wrap will let the bricks slip out easily when they are dry.

Make sure your mixture is packed tightly into the tray.

Pour the dirt into your mixing bowl, and add half a cup of water. Cut the grass into small pieces, and add it in. Mix everything together until it looks and feels like soft clay.

1

The Great Wall of China

The longest human-made structure in the world is the Great Wall of China. It was built over the course of 2,000 years using stone, soil, sand, and brick. The wall is 5,500 miles (8,850 km) long.

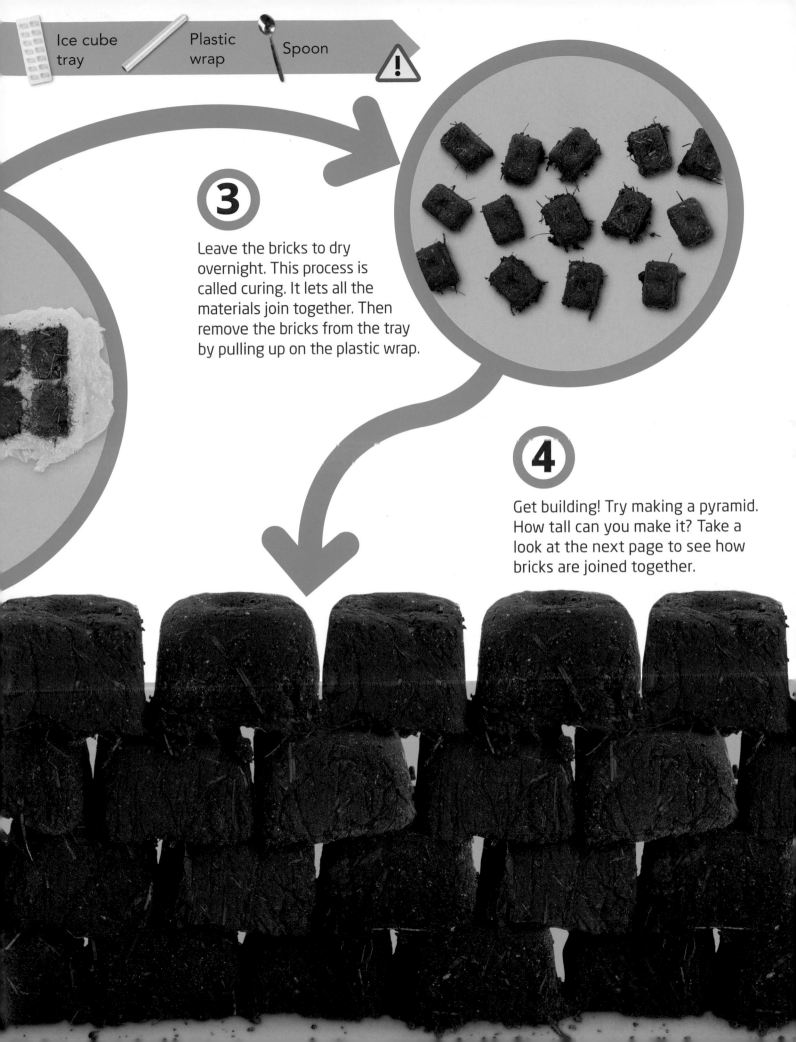

3

Leave the bricks to dry overnight. This process is called curing. It lets all the materials join together. Then remove the bricks from the tray by pulling up on the plastic wrap.

4

Get building! Try making a pyramid. How tall can you make it? Take a look at the next page to see how bricks are joined together.

Take your first sugar cube, and add a small ball of sticky tack to one side.

Repeat step one until you have a row of four sugar cubes. You should have a piece of sticky tack between each cube.

1

Be careful not to press too hard, or the sugar cube will crumble!

2

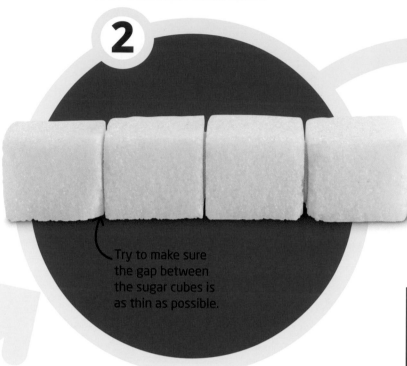

Try to make sure the gap between the sugar cubes is as thin as possible.

Building walls

Using bricks and a special paste called mortar to create structures is called masonry. Mortar is what holds the bricks together. It is usually made of a powdery substance called cement mixed with fine sand and water. You can build your own masonry with sugar cubes and sticky tack (adhesive putty).

3 Now start building upward, putting each cube above and between the two cubes beneath it. Try making a triangle shape.

Using bricks

Many buildings are put together using bricks. Bricks are one of the strongest and longest-lasting materials, which is why they have been used in construction for thousands of years. House bricks are made from clay and baked in an oven to make them hard.

A construction worker using bricks to make a wall

Now try...

Experiment with the cubes to see what else you can make can you build a 3-D pyramid?

How stable is your wall? Do you notice any weak points?

Snap or bend?

When engineers are deciding what materials to use, they have to think about how the materials react to pushing and pulling forces. Try testing out these forces for yourself using a straw and a rubber band.

Cut the straw and rubber band so that they are the same length. Make sure you cut off the bendy part of the straw.

1

The straw stretches a little bit.

The rubber band stretches a long way.

2

Now try pulling the ends of the straw and the rubber band. Does each material stretch or stay the same?

18

Compression and tension

A pushing force on both sides of an object is called compression. A pulling force is called tension. Compression tries to shorten an object, while tension tries to lengthen it.

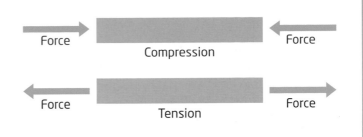

| Force → | Compression | ← Force |

| ← Force | Tension | Force → |

Push and pull forces

3

Next, try pushing the ends of the straw toward each other. Do the same with the rubber band. What happens now?

The straw bends in the middle.

The rubber band curls up.

Now try...

Try pushing and pulling other materials, such as uncooked spaghetti. What happens if you try to make the spaghetti into an arch?

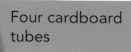

Make sure there are no gaps in the tape, so your materials can't escape.

1 Cover one end of each cardboard tube with tape.

Empty   **Popcorn**   **Gravel**

2 Leave one tube empty, but tape up the other end. Fill each of the remaining tubes with a different material: popcorn, gravel, and salt. Tape up the other ends to keep everything in.

Tubes of strength

Engineers need to know what materials are best for building different things. Wood is great for making small buildings, but it isn't strong enough for skyscrapers and is too heavy to build planes with. Investigating materials will give you a better idea of what they might be useful for.

Now try...

How might other materials react when squashed? If you have more cardboard tubes, you can try filling them with other things. What is the strongest material you can find?

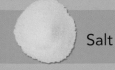
Salt

Strong supports

Different building materials make structures strong or weak. Big structures need to use strong materials. Huge beams called girders are used to support heavy weights. When something presses on a girder, it causes compression. The girder must be able to withstand compression, or it will collapse. Girders are made of a very strong metal called steel.

This bridge is made of steel girders.

Salt

3 Slowly stand on each tube, one at a time. How do the different tubes react? Which is the strongest?

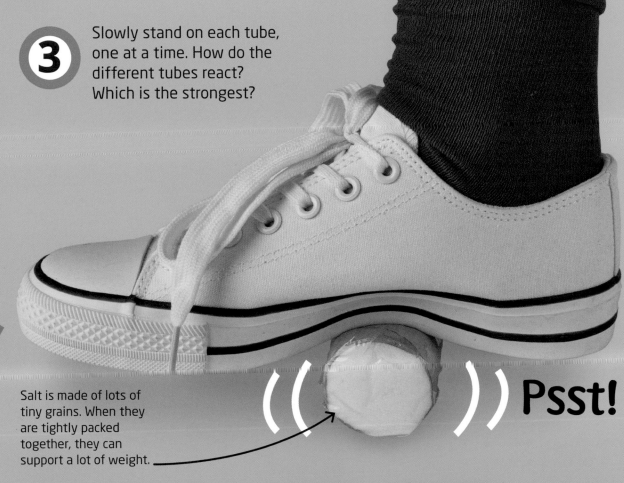

Salt is made of lots of tiny grains. When they are tightly packed together, they can support a lot of weight.

((( )) Psst!

The empty tube collapses completely under the weight of a person.

Pfffftt!

Popcorn is quite soft, so it gets squashed when you stand on it.

Squash!

Gravel has larger pieces than salt. It shifts around a little but is still very strong.

Crunch!

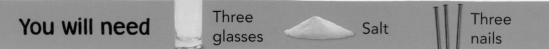

No water   **Water**   **Salt water**

1 Line up your three glasses, and fill two with water. Mix a teaspoon of salt into one of the glasses of water. Then put a nail in each glass.

Rusty
nails

When metal meets oxygen and water, a reaction happens. The reaction causes reddish-brown flakes to appear on the surface of the metal— this is called rust. See metal rusting for yourself using water and nails.

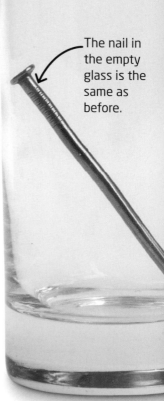

The nail in the empty glass is the same as before.

No water

Stopping rust

To stop metals from rusting, people often cover them in a layer of another metal called zinc. Putting a coating on metal helps stop oxygen from coming into contact with the metal's surface. Without oxygen, it can't rust. This process is called galvanizing. The zinc acts as a protective barrier—it rusts before the metal underneath does.

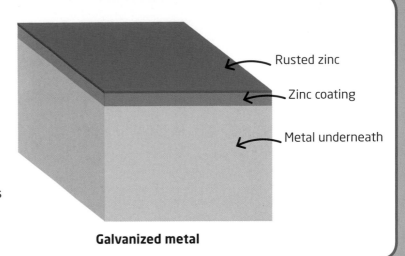

Rusted zinc

Zinc coating

Metal underneath

Galvanized metal

2 Leave the glasses for 24 hours. What do you see on each nail? Which nails have orange and brown dust on them? Try to avoid touching the rusty nails.

The nail in plain water has rusted.

Water

The nail in salt water is completely covered in rust.

Salt water

Mae Jemison

Chemical engineer and astronaut
• Born 1956 • From the United States

Mae Jemison was the first African American woman to travel in space. She went into space in 1992, as the science mission specialist aboard NASA's space shuttle *Endeavour*.

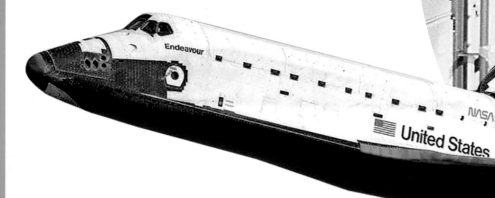

Joining NASA

In 1987, Jemison was accepted into NASA's astronaut program. She made a trip into space on *Endeavour* in 1992. Jemison spent eight days onboard *Endeavour,* traveling around and around the earth.

Space Shuttle *Endeavour*

Space experiments

Jemison took four female frogs with her on her trip to space. While onboard *Endeavour,* she carried out an experiment to see if the frogs could lay eggs in space—and they could! This experiment was important because it suggested that maybe humans could have babies in space too.

When the tadpoles hatched in space, they swam around in circles and spirals.

After NASA

Jemison left NASA in 1993, but her career didn't end there. She set up a science research company and a group that runs international science camps for high-school children. Jemison is also involved in 100 Year Starship, a project to fund research into sending crewed spacecraft outside our solar system.

Jemison aboard Endeavour

Get your adult to carefully pour the lumpy mixture through a sieve into a bowl.

2

Ask an adult to help with the pouring.

You won't need this liquid.

1

Ask an adult to heat 8½ oz (240 ml) of milk until it's almost boiling. Add a few drops of food coloring, then pour in the vinegar, and watch as the milk shrinks into curds.

Make your own plastic

Plastics are materials that can be easily shaped into solid objects and do not rot over time. When plastics are recycled, they are melted down and remolded into different items. Most plastics are made from oil, but some are found in nature. In this experiment you can make your own plastic from milk.

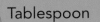 
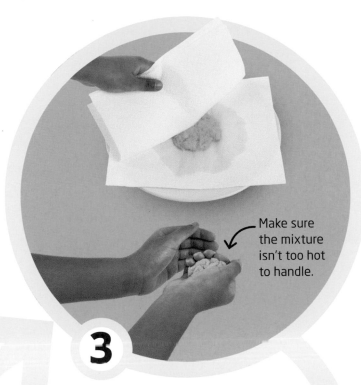

Make sure the mixture isn't too hot to handle.

3

When the mixture has cooled, pat it with paper towels to get out any extra liquid. Next, knead it together using your hands, until it makes one big lump.

Make it again

Recycling takes used products that we are going to throw away and makes them into new things. Plastics get shredded, washed, melted down into pellets, and then reformed. Plastic, paper, and glass can all be recycled.

Shredded plastic

4

Flatten out the mixture on a piece of aluminum foil. Cut it using cookie cutters, or shape it with your hands. Then leave it to dry for two days.

Your finished plastic will be hard and slightly shiny.

Leave your plastic on the foil to dry.

27

Stephanie Kwolek

Chemical engineer
Born 1923 • From the United States

Stephanie Kwolek was an American chemist who experimented with chemicals to make new materials. Her inventions help keep firefighters, police officers, and soldiers safe.

Kevlar

Kwolek invented Kevlar in 1965. It is a very strong but lightweight material that has saved thousands of lives. Kevlar is used to make many different things, including bulletproof vests, protective gloves, helmets, space suits and spacecraft, and aircraft.

Kevlar is what makes these vests bulletproof.

Sheets of Kevlar can be put on almost anything to make it stronger.

Kevlar is used in gloves for extra protection.

New materials

A lot of Kwolek's work involved creating and researching polymers. A polymer is a chain of thousands of atoms. Polymers can be found naturally in plants, but Kwolek researched artificial polymers, like plastic, while trying to come up with ideas for new materials.

Plastic is a polymer. It is useful for lots of things, from water bottles to toys.

Fireproof fabric

In the 1960s, Kwolek helped create a material that protected against fire and heat. It is called Nomex. This material is still used to make uniforms for firefighters, astronauts, and race-car drivers.

Kevlar makes bicycle tires lighter and tougher.

Some canoes are made of Kevlar, making them light and strong.

Nomex keeps firefighters safe in very hot places.

Police officers wear helmets made from Kevlar to protect their heads.

Ropes made with Kevlar are used in space and under the sea.

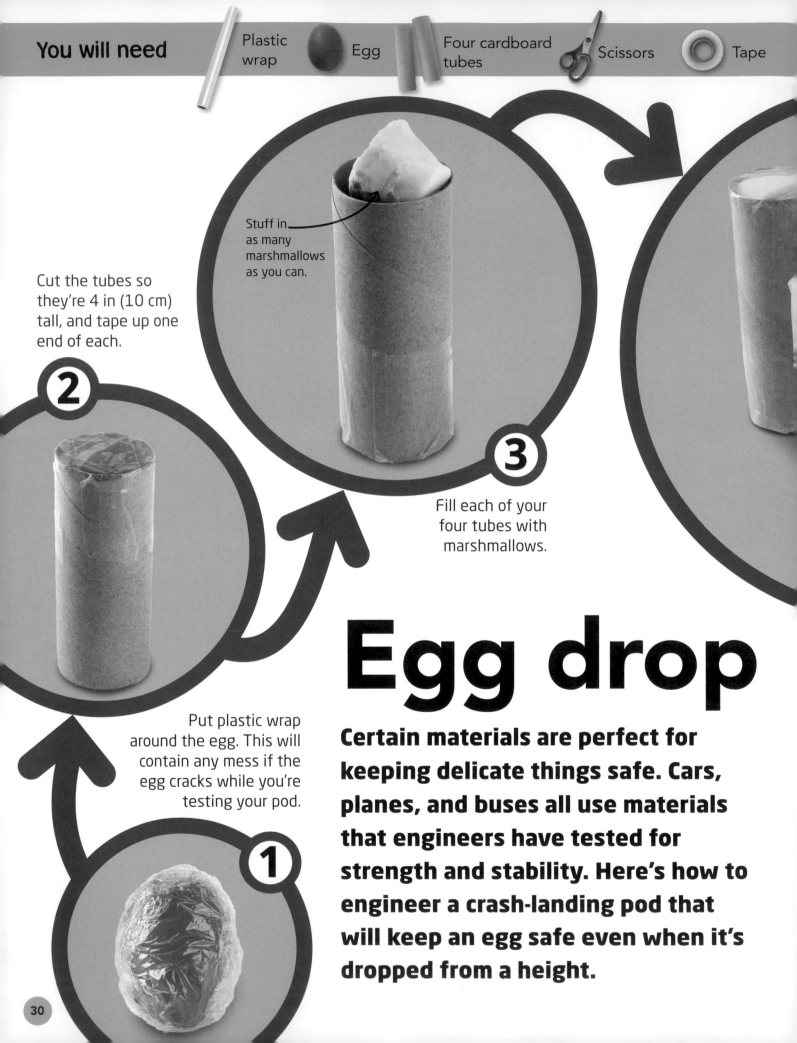

Stuff in as many marshmallows as you can.

Cut the tubes so they're 4 in (10 cm) tall, and tape up one end of each.

2

3

Fill each of your four tubes with marshmallows.

Put plastic wrap around the egg. This will contain any mess if the egg cracks while you're testing your pod.

1

Egg drop

Certain materials are perfect for keeping delicate things safe. Cars, planes, and buses all use materials that engineers have tested for strength and stability. Here's how to engineer a crash-landing pod that will keep an egg safe even when it's dropped from a height.

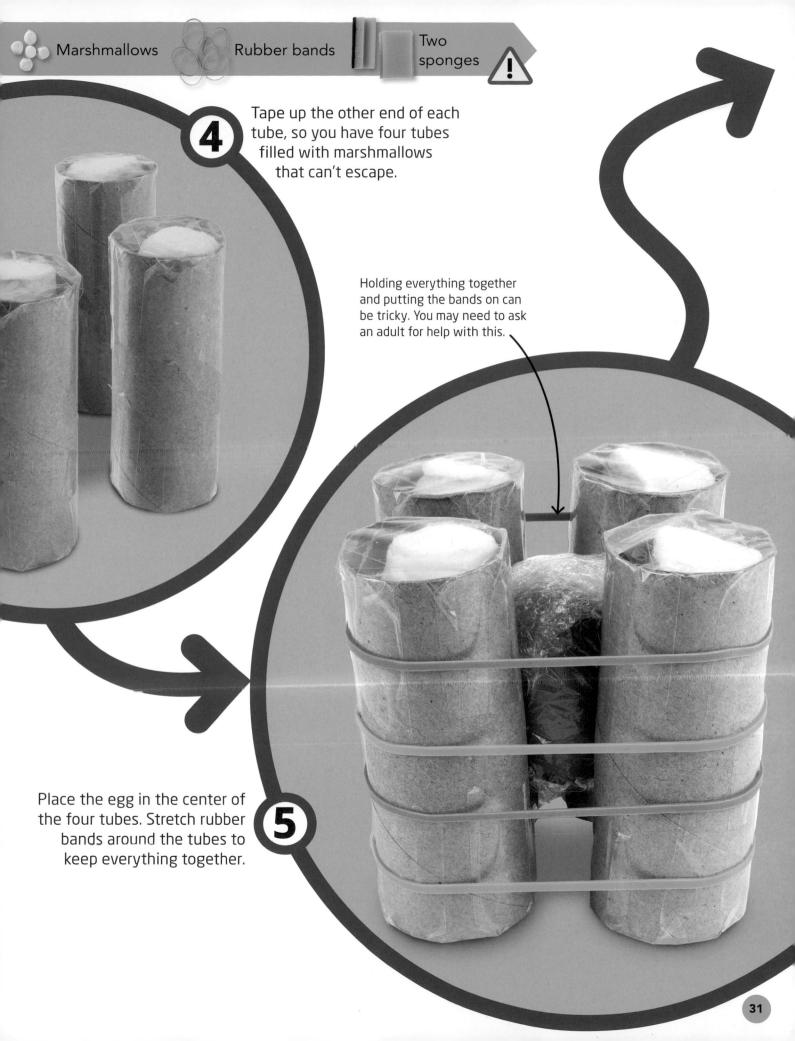

4 Tape up the other end of each tube, so you have four tubes filled with marshmallows that can't escape.

Holding everything together and putting the bands on can be tricky. You may need to ask an adult for help with this.

5 Place the egg in the center of the four tubes. Stretch rubber bands around the tubes to keep everything together.

31

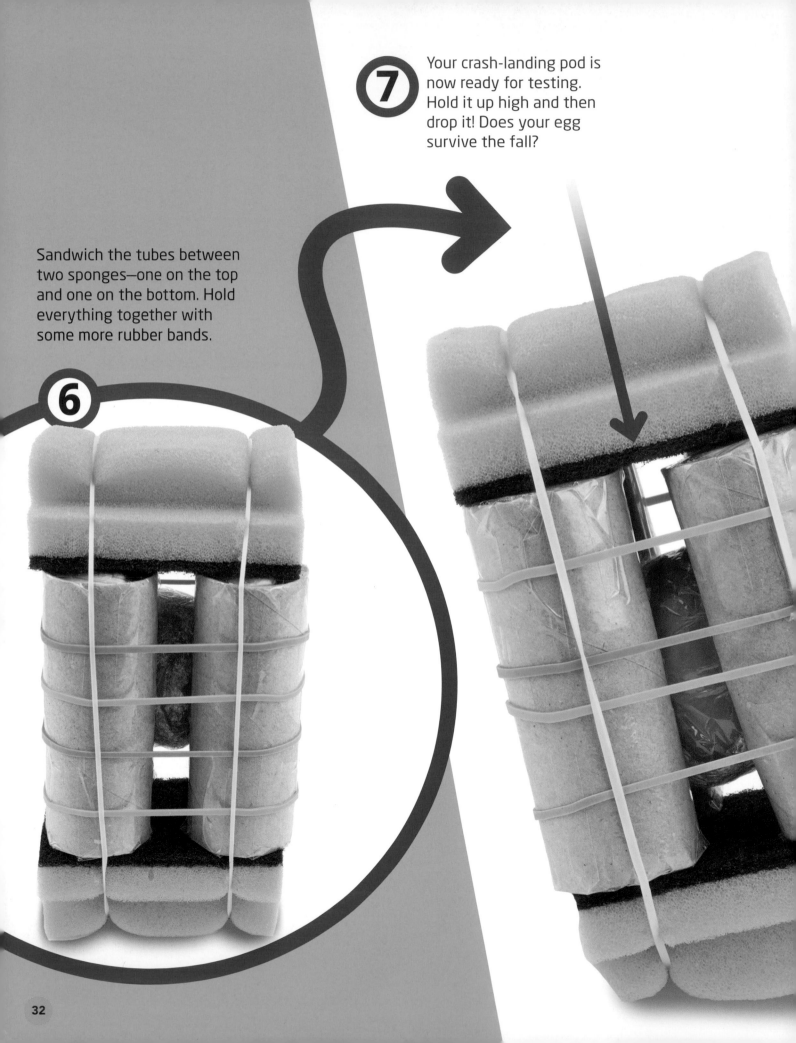

Sandwich the tubes between two sponges—one on the top and one on the bottom. Hold everything together with some more rubber bands.

6

7 Your crash-landing pod is now ready for testing. Hold it up high and then drop it! Does your egg survive the fall?

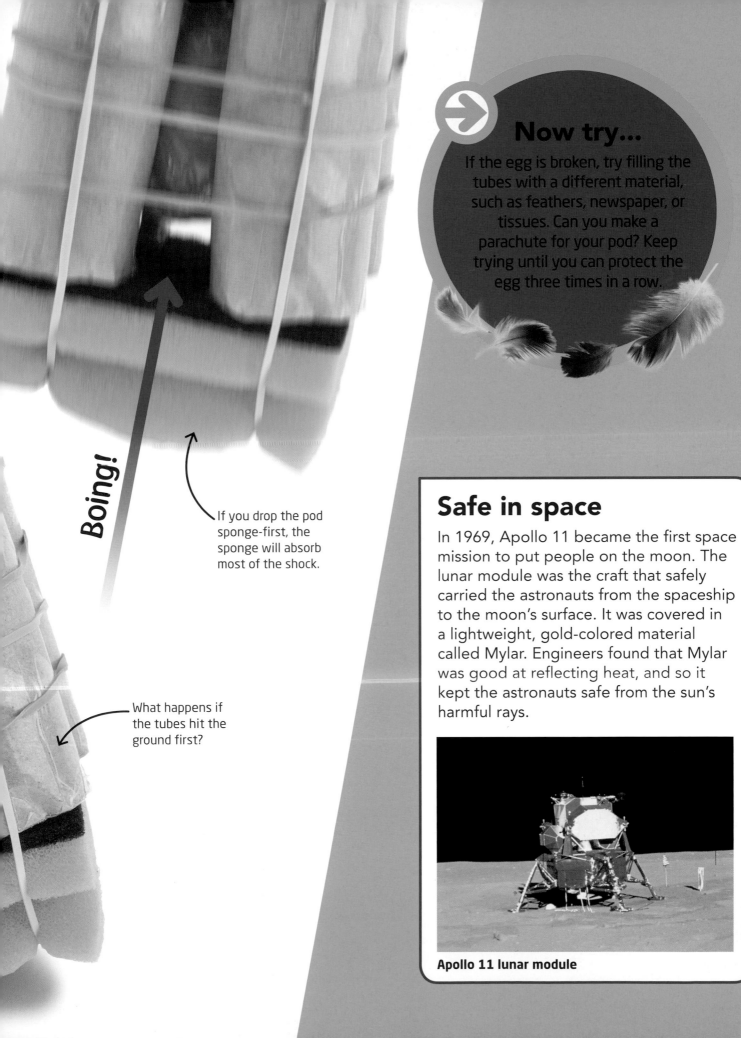

Boing!

If you drop the pod sponge-first, the sponge will absorb most of the shock.

What happens if the tubes hit the ground first?

➡ **Now try...**

If the egg is broken, try filling the tubes with a different material, such as feathers, newspaper, or tissues. Can you make a parachute for your pod? Keep trying until you can protect the egg three times in a row.

Safe in space

In 1969, Apollo 11 became the first space mission to put people on the moon. The lunar module was the craft that safely carried the astronauts from the spaceship to the moon's surface. It was covered in a lightweight, gold-colored material called Mylar. Engineers found that Mylar was good at reflecting heat, and so it kept the astronauts safe from the sun's harmful rays.

Apollo 11 lunar module

Towers

Bridges

Roads

Railroads

Power plants

Buildings

Houses

Arches

Strong structures

Engineers invent, design, and build all kinds of structures, from roads to skyscrapers. These structures must do the job they are designed for, while also being strong and stable enough to last for a long time.

Skyscrapers

Tunnels

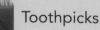
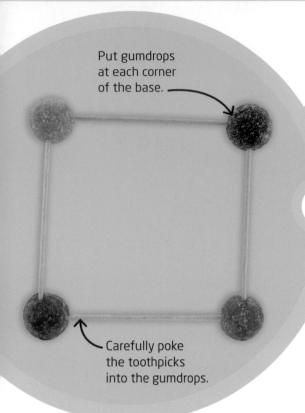

Put gumdrops at each corner of the base.

Carefully poke the toothpicks into the gumdrops.

1

Your aim is to make the tallest tower possible with your gumdrops. It must not fall over! Start by building a base.

You may notice the toothpicks starting to bend as the tower gets taller.

Now begin to build upward. How high can you go before the tower falls over?

2

Build a gumdrop tower

When engineers build a tower, they need to make sure it will be strong and stable. To test their ideas, they often create small-scale models. You can do this using toothpicks and a few gumdrops.

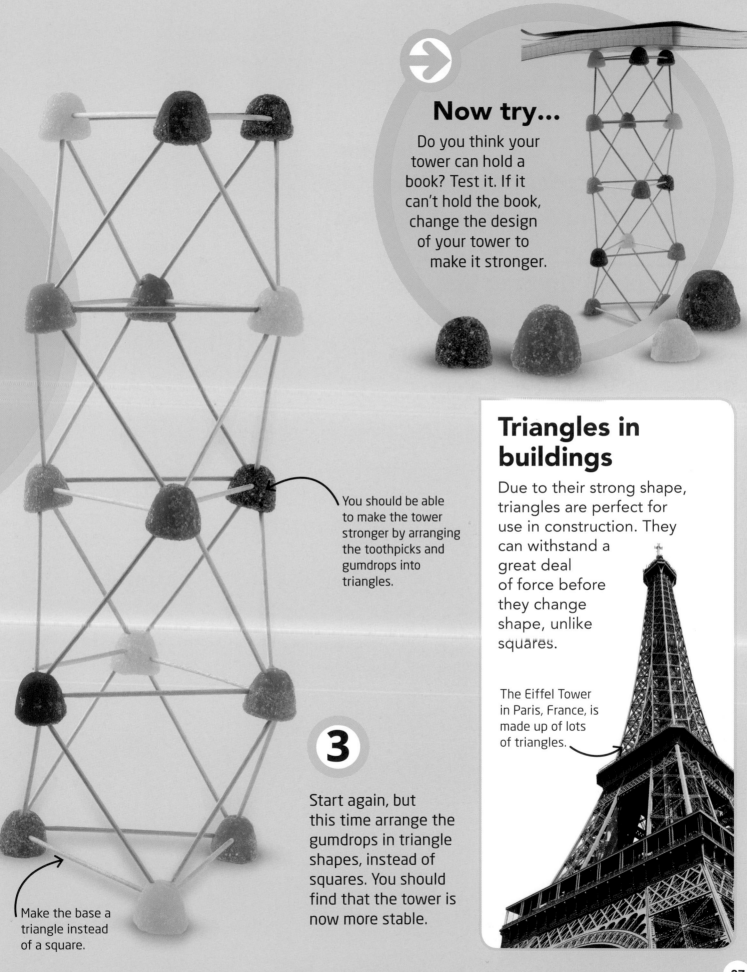

Now try...

Do you think your tower can hold a book? Test it. If it can't hold the book, change the design of your tower to make it stronger.

You should be able to make the tower stronger by arranging the toothpicks and gumdrops into triangles.

Triangles in buildings

Due to their strong shape, triangles are perfect for use in construction. They can withstand a great deal of force before they change shape, unlike squares.

The Eiffel Tower in Paris, France, is made up of lots of triangles.

3

Start again, but this time arrange the gumdrops in triangle shapes, instead of squares. You should find that the tower is now more stable.

Make the base a triangle instead of a square.

Bridges

For thousands of years, people have been crossing over things using bridges. Although most bridges look similar, there are important differences in the way they are built. Many have to be strong enough to carry millions of cars, people, or trains every year.

Bascule

Some bridges need to allow large ships to pass beneath them. To do this, they can raise sections of the bridge, a little like a castle's drawbridge.

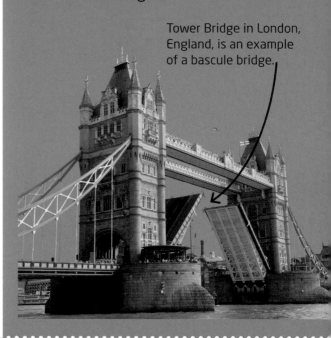

Tower Bridge in London, England, is an example of a bascule bridge.

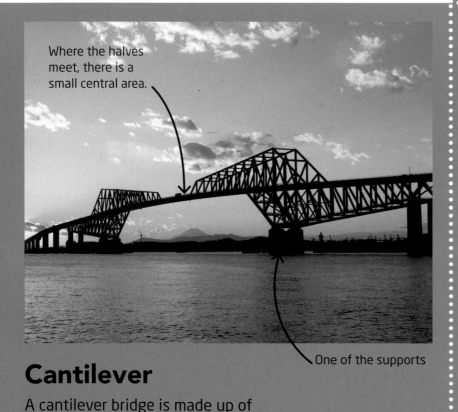

Where the halves meet, there is a small central area.

One of the supports

Cantilever

A cantilever bridge is made up of two halves, which are each supported at only one end. They are connected in the middle.

Straight
steel cables

Cable-stayed

This type of bridge is held up by incredibly
strong steel cables. They are attached to
tall towers that rise high above the road.

Suspension

Two large steel cables, attached to
two large towers, suspend this type
of bridge in the air. Suspension bridges
weigh less than other bridges, so they
can cover great distances.

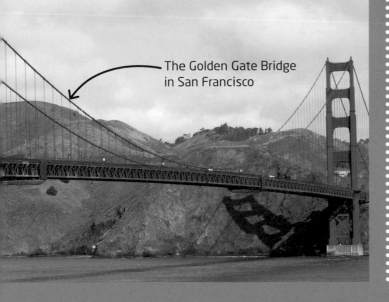

The Golden Gate Bridge
in San Francisco

Beam

Beam bridges are one
of the simplest types
of bridges. They are
supported from below
by columns placed in
the ground, riverbed,
or seabed.

Donghai Bridge in
China is 20 miles
(32.5 km) long.

Sydney Harbour
Bridge, Australia

Arch

These bridges are connected to the
banks on either side of the river by
an arch. Arches are incredibly strong
structures, which is why they are used
so often in architecture.

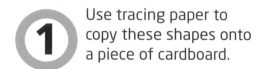
Cardboard arch

Arches let engineers build things with gaps in them, such as windows or space for water to pass through. They are useful because they spread out the weight they are carrying, unlike square shapes. Try shaping an arch of your own!

1 Use tracing paper to copy these shapes onto a piece of cardboard.

Cut out one copy of the large shape.

Cut out 12 copies of the small shape.

Arch bridges

Arch bridges have been built for thousands of years. The first ones were built by the ancient Romans. The stones must be cut into exactly the right wedge shapes to form an arch. Some of these arch bridges are still standing today.

Roman arch bridge in Rimini, Italy

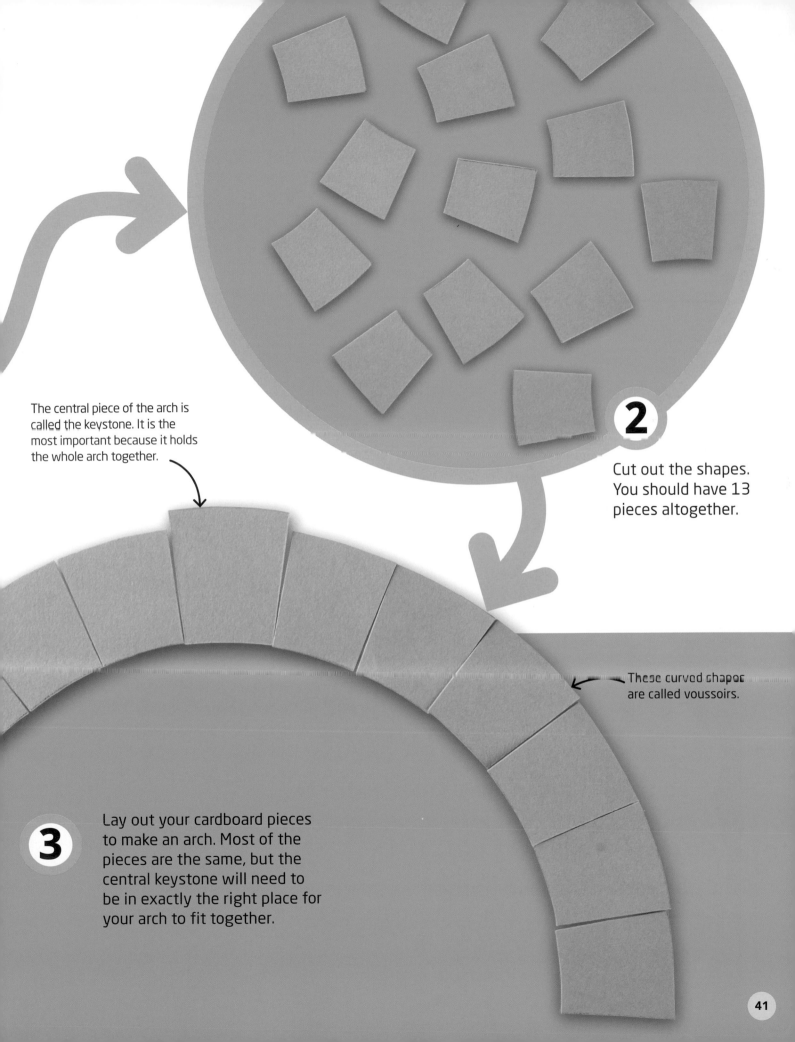

The central piece of the arch is called the keystone. It is the most important because it holds the whole arch together.

2 Cut out the shapes. You should have 13 pieces altogether.

These curved shapes are called voussoirs.

3 Lay out your cardboard pieces to make an arch. Most of the pieces are the same, but the central keystone will need to be in exactly the right place for your arch to fit together.

Next, stick the tubes together to make a series of squares.

2

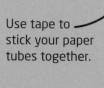

Use tape to stick your paper tubes together.

1

Roll up each piece of paper lengthwise into a narrow tube. Use tape at each end and in the middle to keep it from unrolling.

Skyscraper structures

When engineers don't have much space to build on, they look up! Skyscrapers are built from light materials and have to be strong enough to stay standing when extreme weather strikes. Why not make your own skyscraper tower?

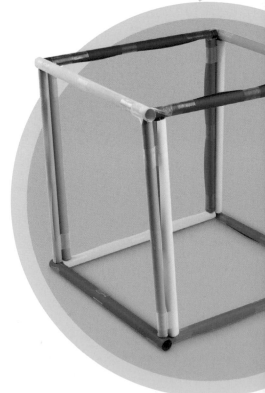

Mega towers

Skyscrapers allow a lot of buildings to fit into small spaces and are the perfect way to build in cities. To make them stable during earthquakes, many skyscrapers are built with flexible materials and have bases that can move slightly.

Dubai is home to many skyscrapers.

Try to make the upright sections point straight up—wobbly towers fall over.

3 Tape four of your squares together to make a cube.

Build more cubes and stack them on top of each other. Then tape them together. How high can your tower get before it falls?

4

Fazlur Rahman Khan

Engineer and architect • Born 1929 • From Bangladesh

Fazlur Rahman Khan changed the way skyscrapers are built, making them taller, safer, and cheaper with his "tubular design." He used lightweight concrete and other new materials. Khan worked with other engineers and architects in the United States, creating some of the most famous buildings in the world.

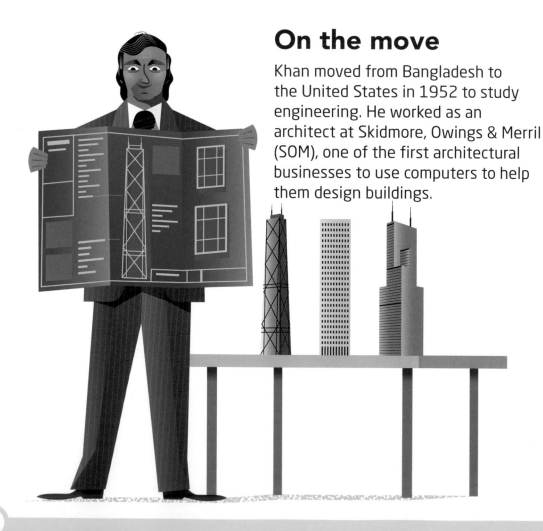

On the move

Khan moved from Bangladesh to the United States in 1952 to study engineering. He worked as an architect at Skidmore, Owings & Merril (SOM), one of the first architectural businesses to use computers to help them design buildings.

Tubular designs

Khan's big idea was a "tubular design" that made skyscrapers stronger, taller, and more stable. This design meant that his skyscrapers were like tall, square tubes with strong supports on the outside. Almost all modern skyscrapers are now designed this way.

The Hajj Terminal, Saudi Arabia

Khan's John Hancock Center in Chicago has 100 stories and is 1,127 ft (343.5 m) tall.

The outside frame is made of steel crosses to make it stronger.

Airport terminal

The Hajj Terminal at King Abdulaziz International Airport was designed by Khan. He planned it to look like tents in the deserts of North Africa and the Middle East.

In 1972, Khan was awarded "Construction's Man of the Year."

Make sure the tape is tightly wrapped around the tubes.

Make sure the towels are long enough to cover the length of the tunnel.

Building tunnels

A tunnel is very different from a bridge or a road. Instead of going above or along the ground, it is hidden beneath the surface. Tunnels can be used for wires and water pipes or for vehicles, such as trains and cars.

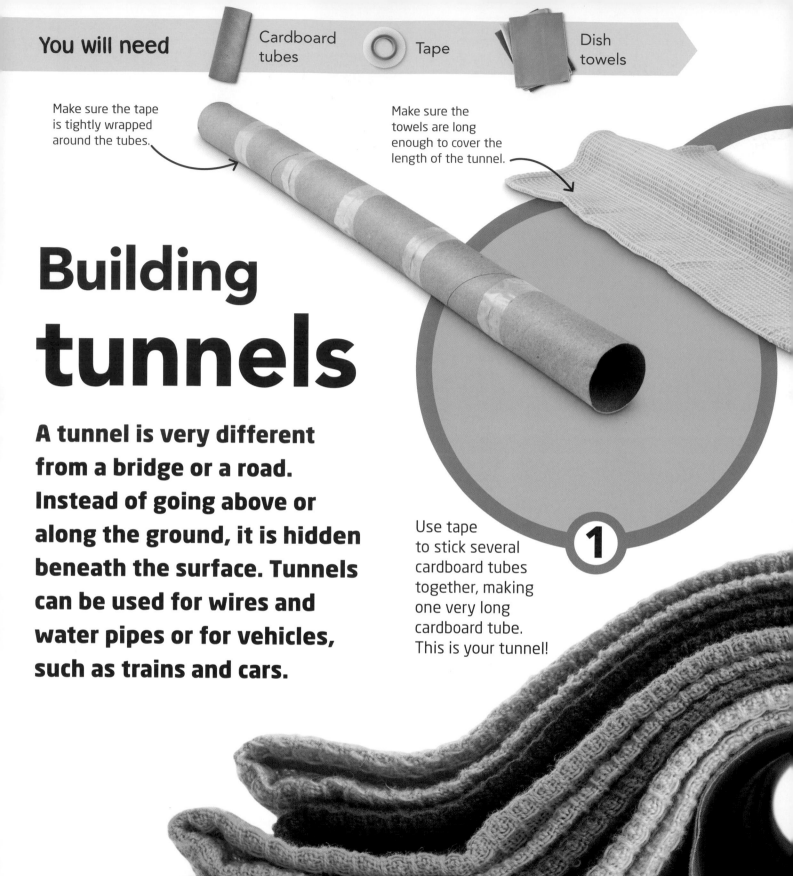

1 Use tape to stick several cardboard tubes together, making one very long cardboard tube. This is your tunnel!

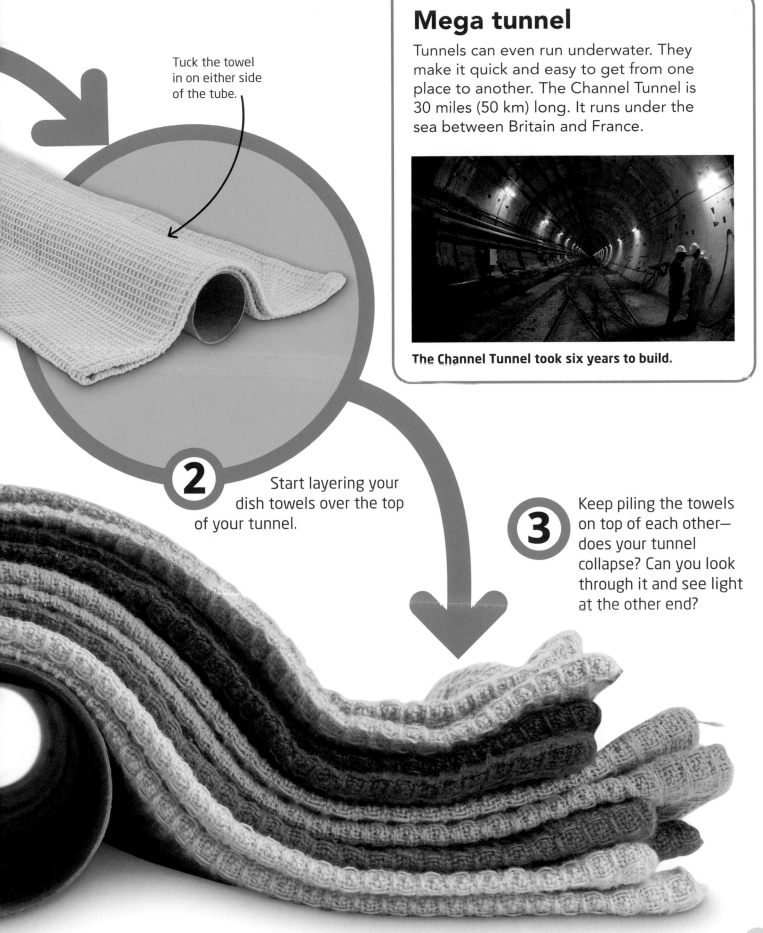

Tuck the towel in on either side of the tube.

Mega tunnel

Tunnels can even run underwater. They make it quick and easy to get from one place to another. The Channel Tunnel is 30 miles (50 km) long. It runs under the sea between Britain and France.

The Channel Tunnel took six years to build.

2 Start layering your dish towels over the top of your tunnel.

3 Keep piling the towels on top of each other—does your tunnel collapse? Can you look through it and see light at the other end?

Set out a 12 in (30 cm) piece of cardboard. On top of it, spread out a sand road and a gravel road, leaving space for a cardboard road at the end.

1

Making roads

People have built roads for thousands of years. They help us get from one place to another, quickly and easily. Try testing out different materials to see which ones make the best roads.

The gravel moves around but is easier to get over than sand.

Smooth cardboard is easy to move on.

Friction

Friction pulls in the opposite direction that something is moving in, making moving objects slow down. There is friction whenever two surfaces rub against each other—for example, a car's tires on a road. The smoother the rubbing objects are the less friction they create. In the experiment, the cardboard road is easiest to travel on because it has the least friction.

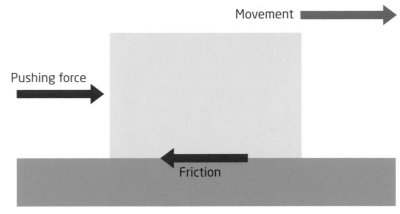

Movement

Pushing force

Friction

Moving surfaces When a pushing force is applied to an object, the object moves. Friction happens where the two moving surfaces meet.

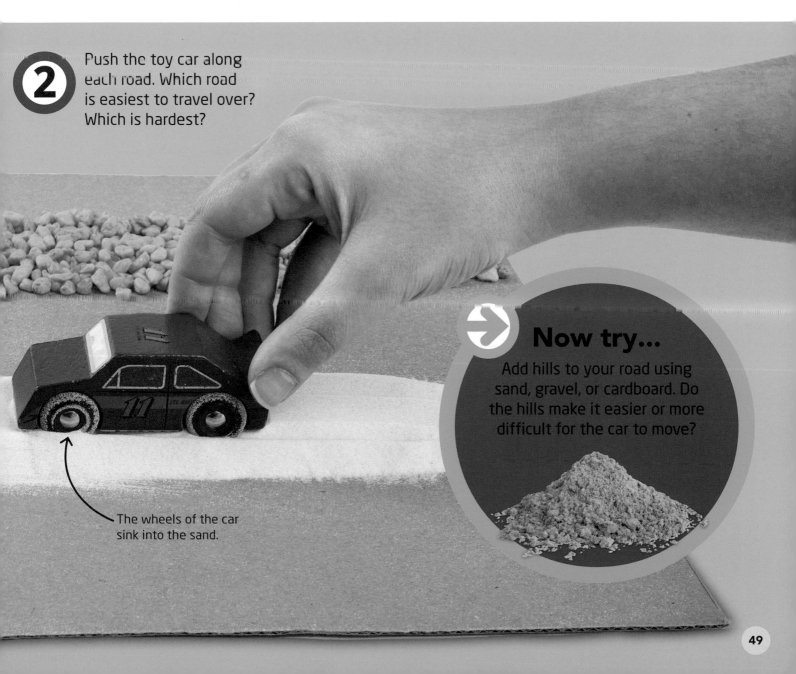

2 Push the toy car along each road. Which road is easiest to travel over? Which is hardest?

The wheels of the car sink into the sand.

Now try...

Add hills to your road using sand, gravel, or cardboard. Do the hills make it easier or more difficult for the car to move?

Isambard Kingdom Brunel

Structural and civil engineer
• Born 1806 • From Britain

Isambard Kingdom Brunel is celebrated as one of the greatest engineers in history. He lived and worked in a time of great change called the Industrial Revolution. His works include bridges, railroads, steamships, and tunnels.

Great Western Railway

In 1833 Brunel began working on a new railroad between Bristol and London in Britain. The railroad was called the Great Western Railway, which crossed over bridges and through tunnels. Queen Victoria took her first ever train journey on it in 1842.

Brilliant bridges

Brunel designed bridges that are still standing today. He won a competition to design a bridge that would cross the River Avon in Bristol, England. This is the Clifton Suspension Bridge. It stands 301 ft (101 m) above the river.

The Clifton Suspension Bridge

The SS *Great Eastern*

Sturdy steamships

In the 1830s, Brunel designed steamships that could sail across oceans, taking people to New York and Sydney, Australia. His ships, the SS *Great Britain* and SS *Great Eastern,* could cross oceans faster than other ships and were the biggest the world had seen at the time.

A steam locomotive traveling on the Great Western Railway, which is still in use today.

Suspension bridge

Suspension bridges are held up by steel cables that hang from huge supports on either side of the bridge. The weight of the bridge is spread along the strong cables. How well will your bridge hold up?

Don't make the hole too big, otherwise the straw will fall out!

1

Using scissors, carefully poke a small hole in the center of each paper towel tube. Make sure the hole is just big enough for a straw to fit inside.

Use tape to stick each tube to the cardboard.

Stick the tubes on one side of your piece of cardboard— you need to leave space for the other half of the bridge.

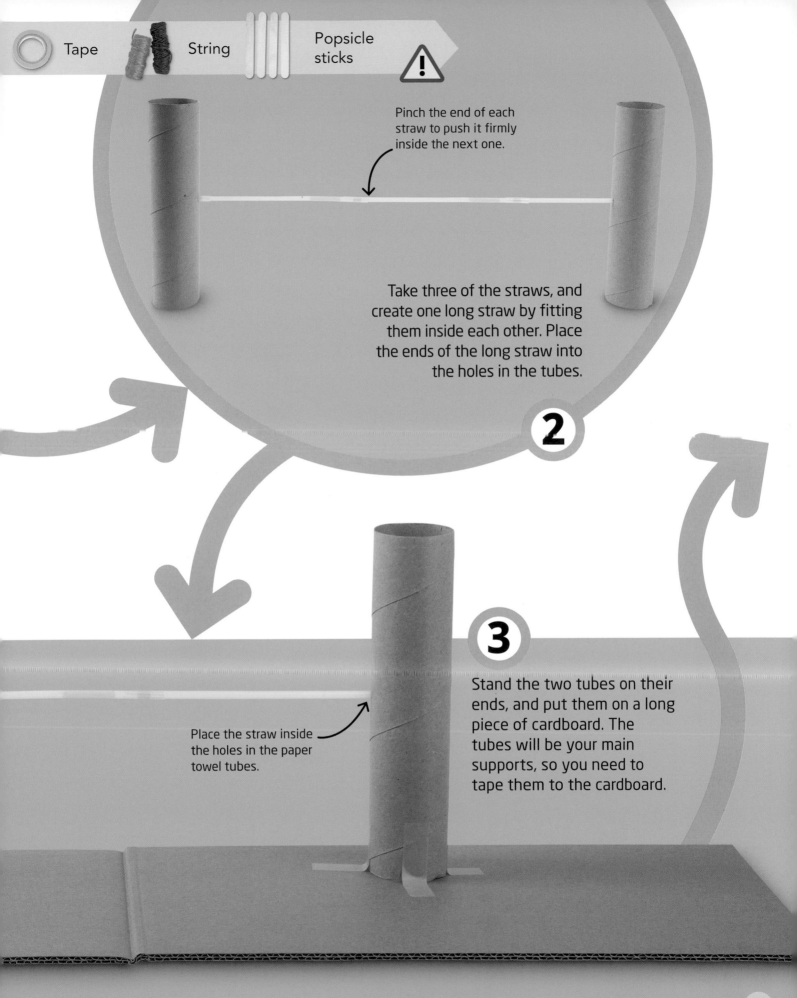

Pinch the end of each straw to push it firmly inside the next one.

Take three of the straws, and create one long straw by fitting them inside each other. Place the ends of the long straw into the holes in the tubes.

2

3

Place the straw inside the holes in the paper towel tubes.

Stand the two tubes on their ends, and put them on a long piece of cardboard. The tubes will be your main supports, so you need to tape them to the cardboard.

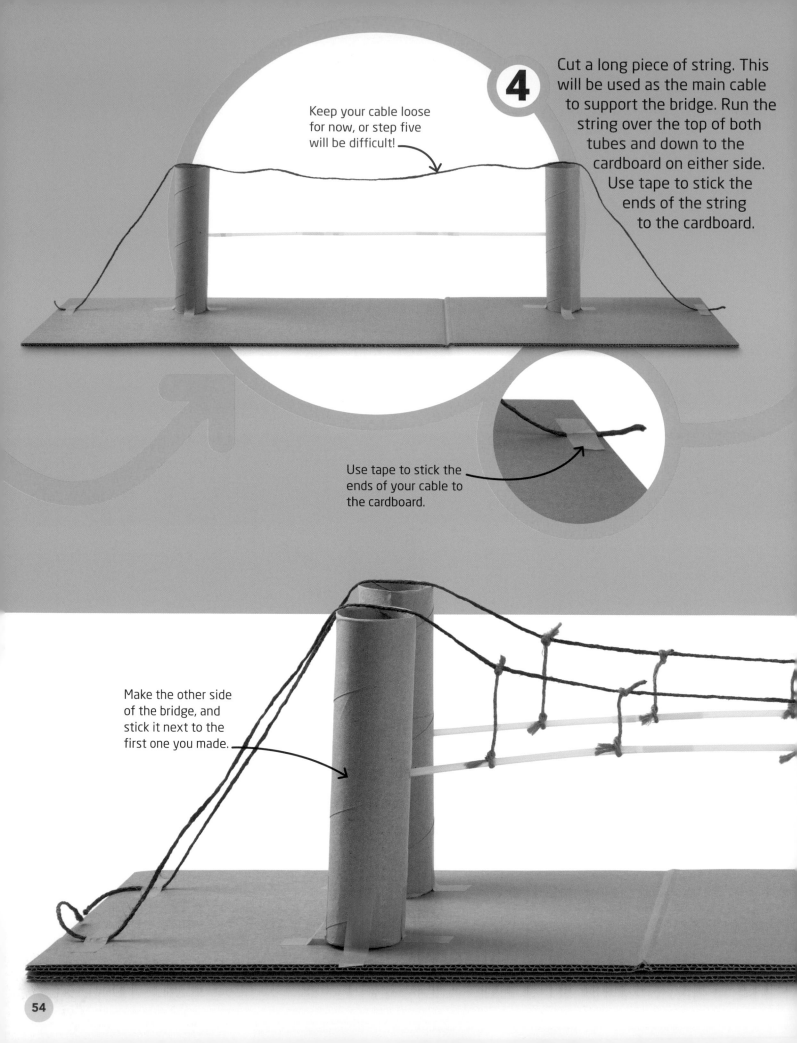

Keep your cable loose for now, or step five will be difficult!

4 Cut a long piece of string. This will be used as the main cable to support the bridge. Run the string over the top of both tubes and down to the cardboard on either side. Use tape to stick the ends of the string to the cardboard.

Use tape to stick the ends of your cable to the cardboard.

Make the other side of the bridge, and stick it next to the first one you made.

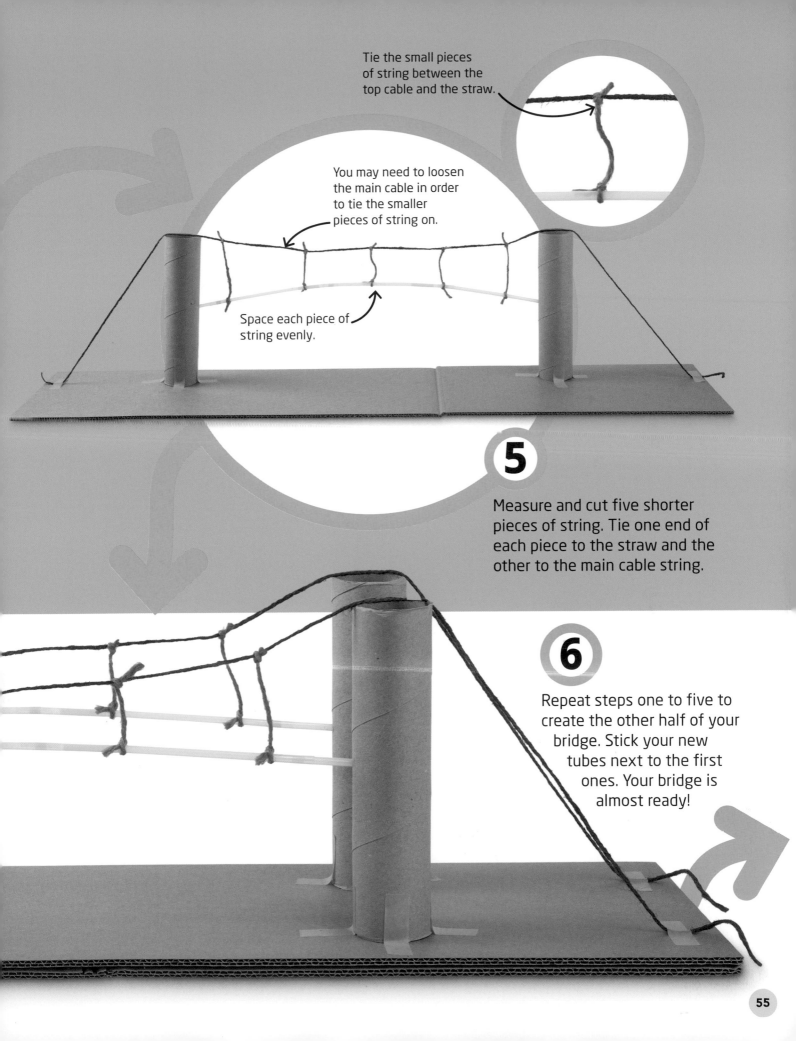

Tie the small pieces of string between the top cable and the straw.

You may need to loosen the main cable in order to tie the smaller pieces of string on.

Space each piece of string evenly.

5

Measure and cut five shorter pieces of string. Tie one end of each piece to the straw and the other to the main cable string.

6

Repeat steps one to five to create the other half of your bridge. Stick your new tubes next to the first ones. Your bridge is almost ready!

55

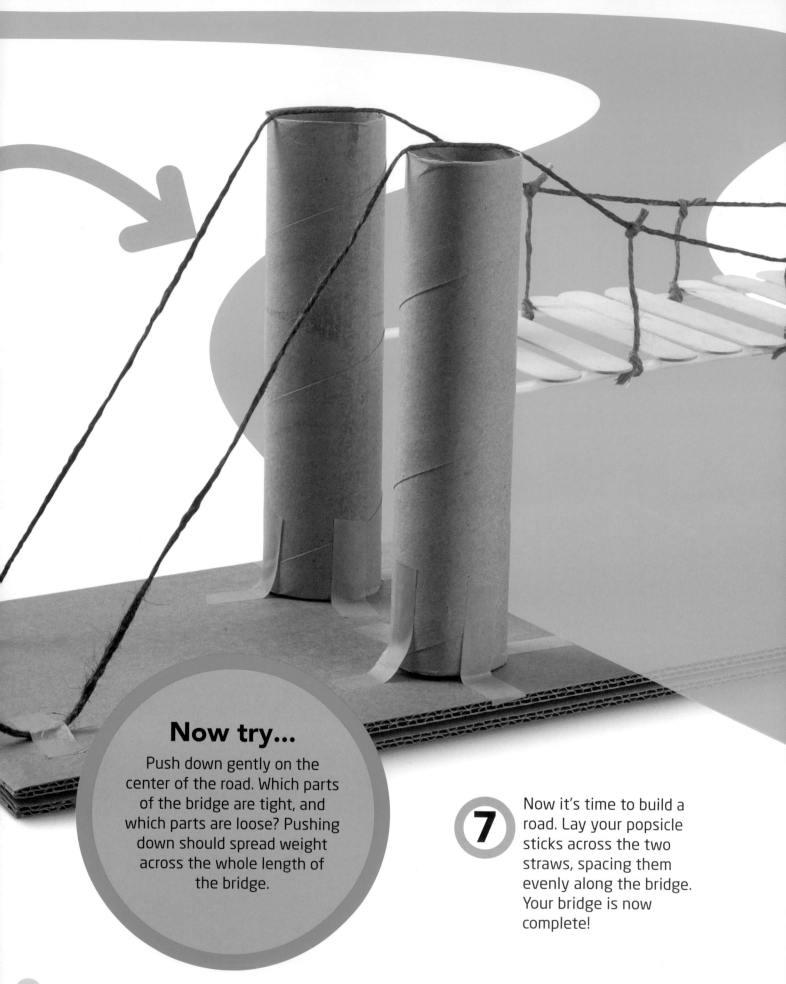

Now try...

Push down gently on the center of the road. Which parts of the bridge are tight, and which parts are loose? Pushing down should spread weight across the whole length of the bridge.

7 Now it's time to build a road. Lay your popsicle sticks across the two straws, spacing them evenly along the bridge. Your bridge is now complete!

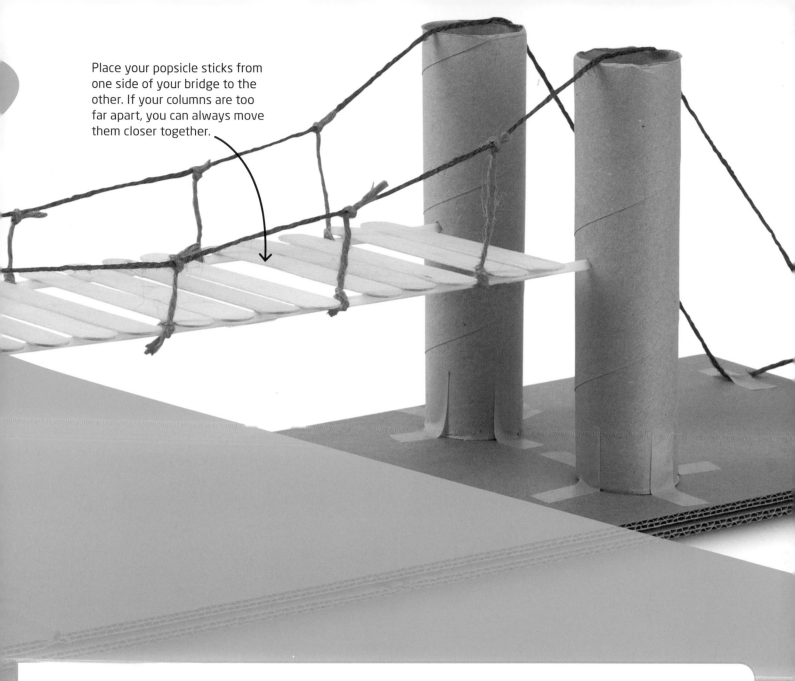

Place your popsicle sticks from one side of your bridge to the other. If your columns are too far apart, you can always move them closer together.

The Golden Gate Bridge

The Golden Gate Bridge is one of the most famous suspension bridges in the world. It is tall enough to allow large ships to travel underneath. The main cable of this bridge is as wide as an adult is tall!

The Golden Gate Bridge is in San Francisco.

Mighty machines

Machines make our lives easier by doing tasks that are too complicated, dangerous, or boring for people to do. Some machines are even built just for us to enjoy.

Cogs

Pulleys

Computers

Gears

Levers

Simple machines

A machine is a tool that is designed to make things easier for humans. Machines reduce the amount of energy, power, and time that it takes to get jobs done.

Pulley

A pulley uses rope and a wheel to pull a heavy load upward. The rope is looped over the wheel, and one end of the rope is attached to the load. The other end of the rope is then pulled down to lift the load up.

Wheel and axle

A wheel and axle can help move things around. The axle is a rod that runs through the wheels. When the axle is turned, the wheels turn too. It is easier to roll heavy objects around than it is to lift or push them.

Wheel

Wedge

A wedge is used to separate, or split, things. It has a sharp, pointed edge that, when brought down on an object, forces that object to crack open.

The axe has split the wood. If the axe wasn't sharp, a bigger force would have been needed to separate the wood.

Screw

A screw creates a downward force that helps hold things together. It has a spiral pattern that runs around the outside of the screw, allowing it to be easily inserted into materials by rotating it.

Turning the screw pushes it downward.

Lever

A lever is a bar that rests on a point called a fulcrum. This lets you lift and move heavy objects. When you push down on one end of the lever, the other end lifts the object up. A seesaw is a lever that lets you lift up the weight of a person on the other end.

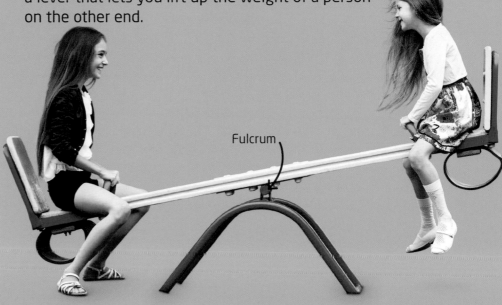

Fulcrum

Gears

A gear is a rotating wheel with teeth, or cogs, on the outer rim. When gears are pushed up against each other and one is turned, the other is forced to move in the opposite direction. Gears can be used to make things turn faster and with more power.

Turning one gear makes the one it is linked to turn too.

Slope

A slope is a slanted surface that connects a low area to a higher one. It is easier to push or pull a heavy object up a slope than it is to lift it.

This box is very heavy. It would be impossible for the person to lift it on their own.

You will need

Ping-pong ball

Tape

Small bowl

Long ruler

Tin can

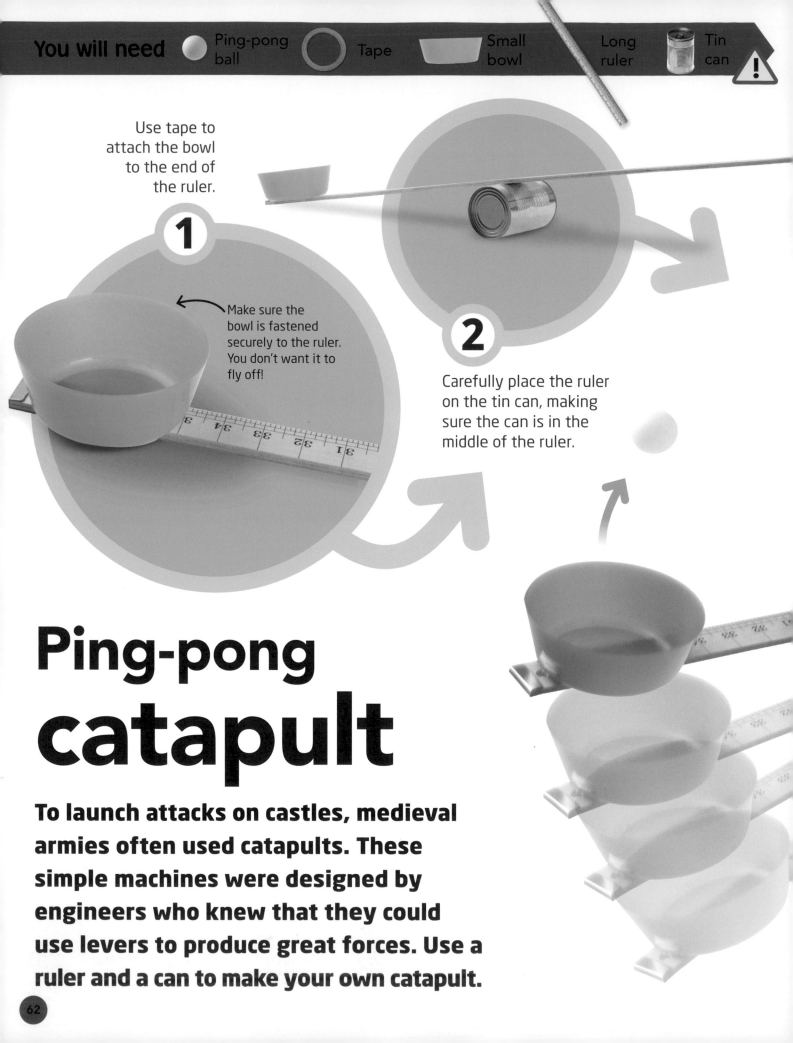

Use tape to attach the bowl to the end of the ruler.

1

Make sure the bowl is fastened securely to the ruler. You don't want it to fly off!

2

Carefully place the ruler on the tin can, making sure the can is in the middle of the ruler.

Ping-pong
catapult

To launch attacks on castles, medieval armies often used catapults. These simple machines were designed by engineers who knew that they could use levers to produce great forces. Use a ruler and a can to make your own catapult.

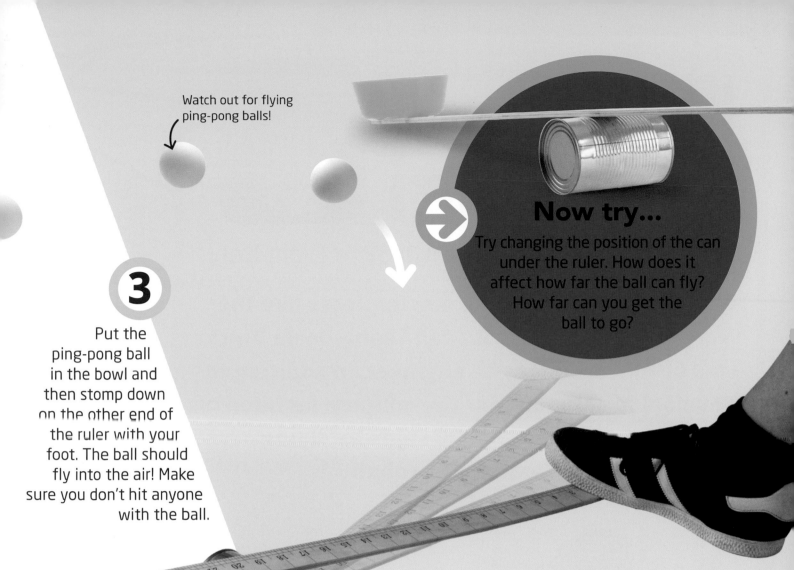

Watch out for flying ping-pong balls!

Now try...

Try changing the position of the can under the ruler. How does it affect how far the ball can fly? How far can you get the ball to go?

3

Put the ping-pong ball in the bowl and then stomp down on the other end of the ruler with your foot. The ball should fly into the air! Make sure you don't hit anyone with the ball.

How do levers work?

Levers are a very simple way of multiplying forces to make tasks easier. The amount by which a lever multiplies a force depends on the distance between your foot, the force created by the lever, and the fulcrum, which is the support in the middle.

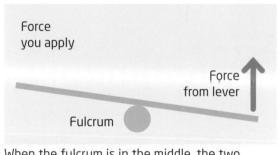

Force you apply

Force from lever

Fulcrum

When the fulcrum is in the middle, the two forces will be equal.

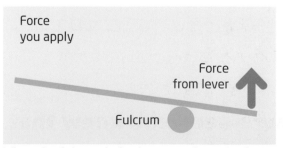

Force you apply

Force from lever

Fulcrum

When the fulcrum is farther away from the force you apply, the resulting force will be bigger.

Leonardo da Vinci

Engineer and artist • Born 1452 • From Italy

When he wasn't painting masterpieces like the *Mona Lisa* or *The Last Supper*, Leonardo da Vinci was busy working as an engineer. In addition to developing catapults for the military, he filled his notebooks with amazing designs for flying machines, tanks, and even a robot!

Da Vinci wrote backward using a mirror so people couldn't steal his ideas.

"I know how... to make an infinite number of bridges."

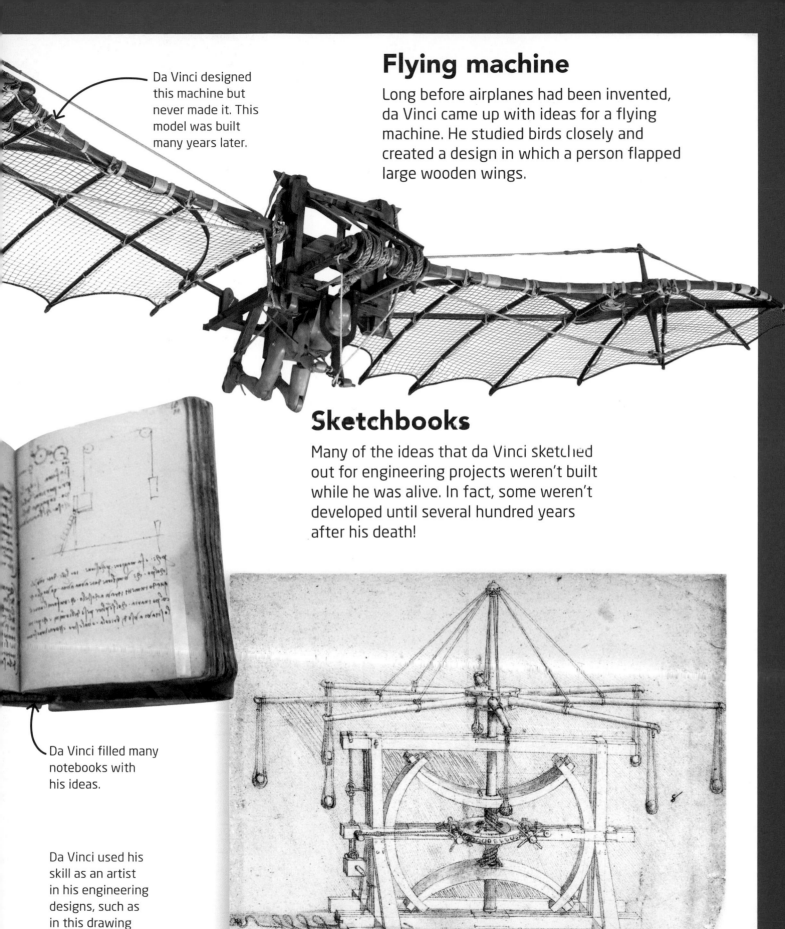

Da Vinci designed this machine but never made it. This model was built many years later.

Flying machine

Long before airplanes had been invented, da Vinci came up with ideas for a flying machine. He studied birds closely and created a design in which a person flapped large wooden wings.

Sketchbooks

Many of the ideas that da Vinci sketched out for engineering projects weren't built while he was alive. In fact, some weren't developed until several hundred years after his death!

Da Vinci filled many notebooks with his ideas.

Da Vinci used his skill as an artist in his engineering designs, such as in this drawing of a catapult.

You will need
Small plastic tub
Sticky tack
Thumbtack
Scissors

Lifting weights

A pulley is a turning wheel with a rope around it. Pulleys let you change the direction of a force—you pull down on the rope at one end in order to lift up something at the other end.

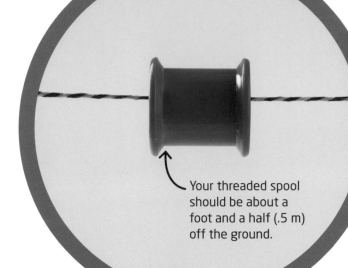

Your threaded spool should be about a foot and a half (.5 m) off the ground.

2

Thread the spool onto your other piece of string. Attach each end to something that won't move, such as a heavy chair. The string needs to be stretched tight.

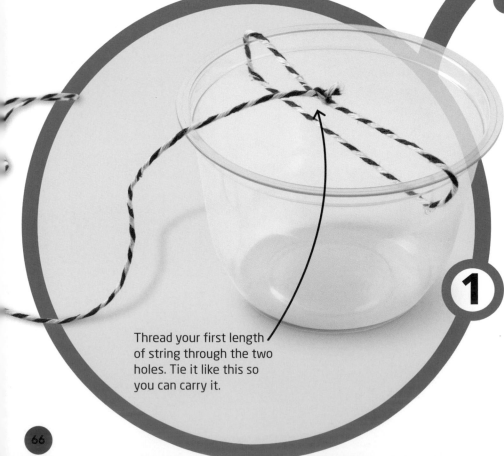

Thread your first length of string through the two holes. Tie it like this so you can carry it.

1

Place two blobs of sticky tack (adhesive putty) opposite each other on the inside of a plastic tub. On each side, carefully push a thumbtack through the plastic into the tack, making two holes. Loop your string through the holes.

Pull!

3

Load the marbles into your plastic tub. Place the tub string over the spool, and pull the loose end down. You can now lift your load using a pulley.

How many marbles can you collect in one load?

Double pulley

If two pulleys are used together, you can lift a heavier weight without having to put in more effort. Using more and more pulleys together would let you lift even heavier loads.

The rope loops around two pulleys.

Pull here.

The weight is lifted up.

Cardboard cogs

Gears move power from one part of a machine to another. They have cogs, or teeth, around the outside. Gears can be used to change the speed, strength, or direction of a force. Test this idea by creating your own set of gears.

1 Trace the big and small gears shown here onto some cardboard, then cut each of them out.

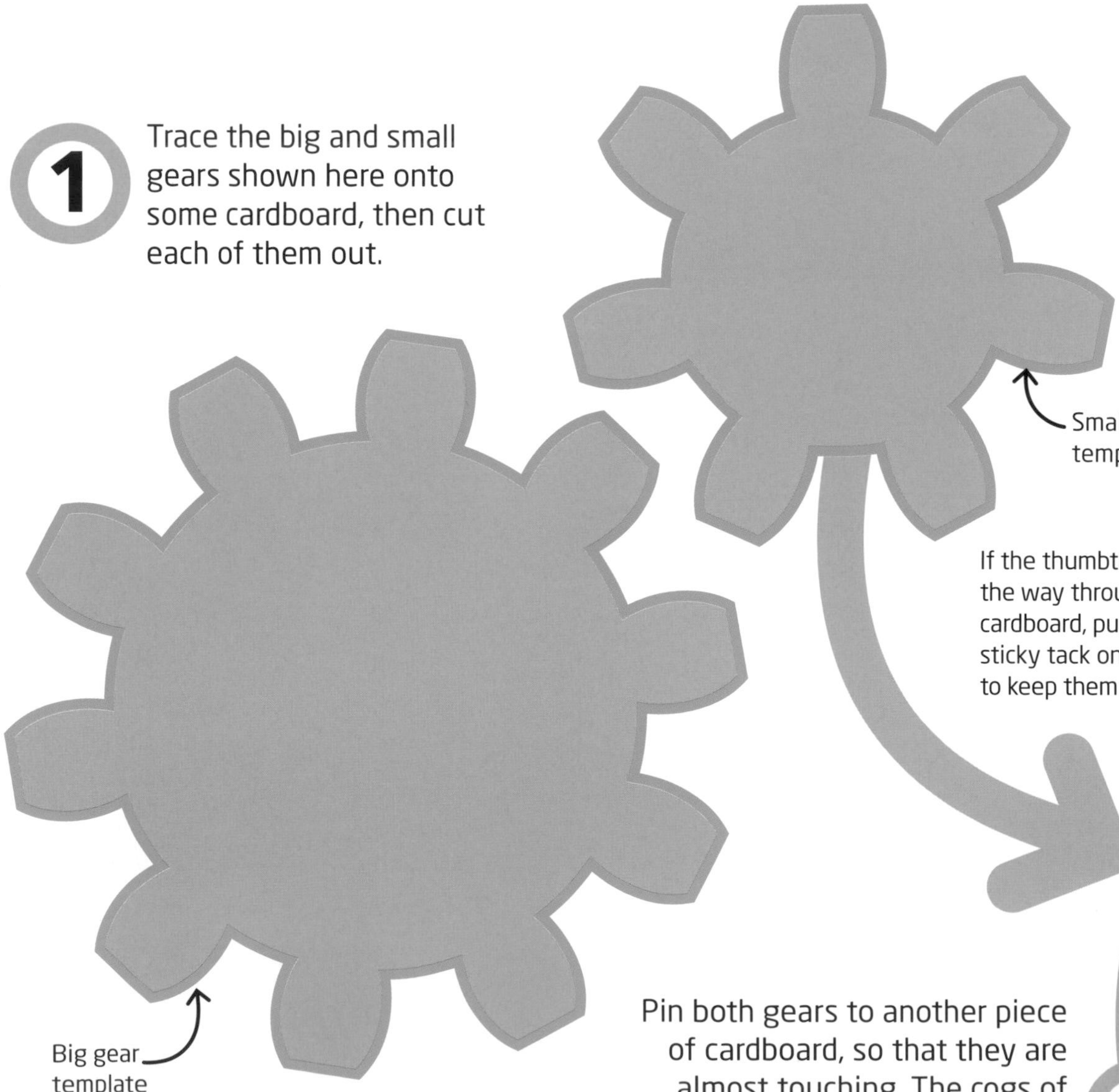

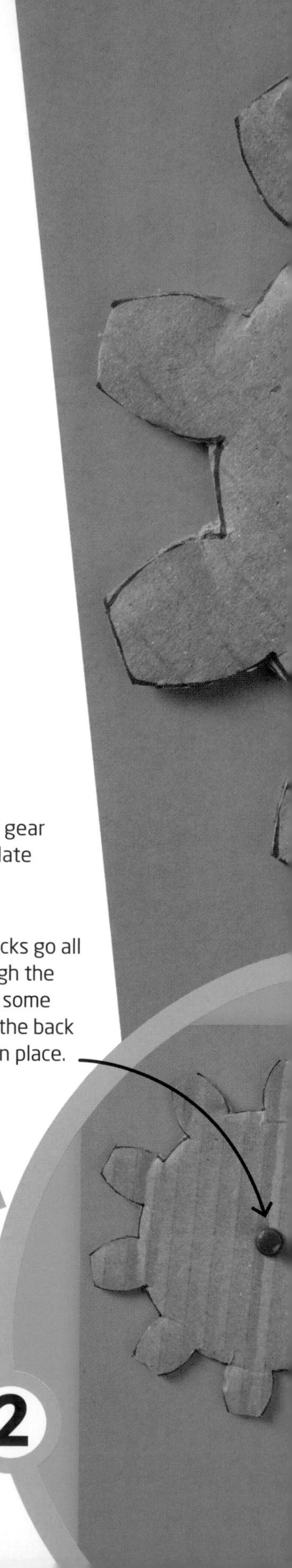

Small gear template

If the thumbtacks go all the way through the cardboard, put some sticky tack on the back to keep them in place.

Big gear template

2 Pin both gears to another piece of cardboard, so that they are almost touching. The cogs of the small gear should fit into the gaps in the big gear.

Sticky tack Thumbtacks

Now try...

See what happens when you add more gears to your set. Can you spin all of them at once?

If you turn this gear clockwise, the other will turn counterclockwise.

Put a thumbtack in the center of each gear.

3 Turn one of the gears, and the other should turn too. What do you notice about the speed and direction of each gear?

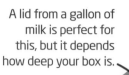

Small cardboard box   Pencil   Thick cardboard   Plastic lid

Draw two lines around the outside of the box to mark where the wheels will go. Make sure the wheels won't hit each other.

1

A lid from a gallon of milk is perfect for this, but it depends how deep your box is.

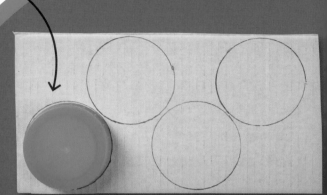

If you find the thick cardboard difficult to cut, ask an adult for help.

Turning wheels

People have been using wheels for thousands of years. Using two wheels connected by a stick called an axle lets you move things around much more easily than lifting them. We still use wheels for many types of transportation today, such as cars, buses, and trucks.

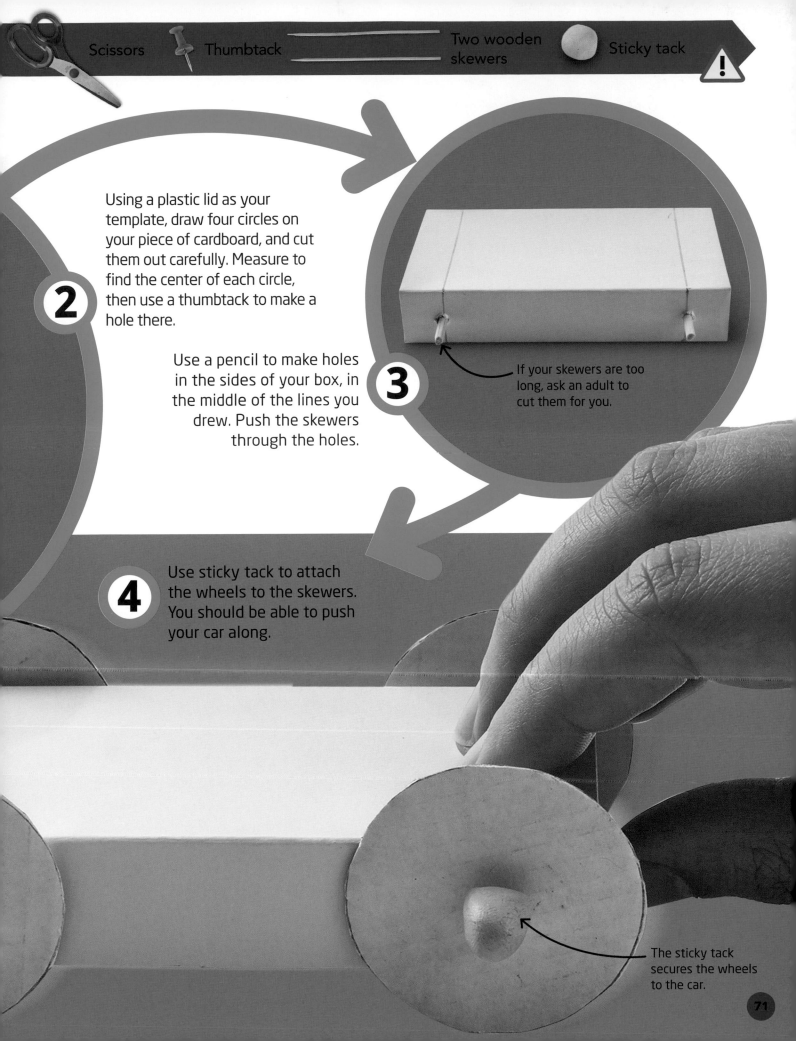

Scissors Thumbtack Two wooden skewers Sticky tack

2 Using a plastic lid as your template, draw four circles on your piece of cardboard, and cut them out carefully. Measure to find the center of each circle, then use a thumbtack to make a hole there.

Use a pencil to make holes in the sides of your box, in the middle of the lines you drew. Push the skewers through the holes.

3

If your skewers are too long, ask an adult to cut them for you.

4 Use sticky tack to attach the wheels to the skewers. You should be able to push your car along.

The sticky tack secures the wheels to the car.

Engines

Most vehicles are powered by engines. Engines burn fuel and release heat, turning the heat energy into movement energy. Most cars have four-stroke engines with four moving parts called pistons.

Types of engines

Not all engines are the same. Big vehicles that need to move fast have the most powerful engines. All engines need fuel to make them go, but different types use different fuels.

Fuel squashed

On the second stroke, the valve closes, and the piston moves up. This squashes the mixture of fuel and air into a smaller space.

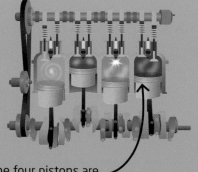

The four pistons are only part of the engine. Each of the pistons goes through the following cycle.

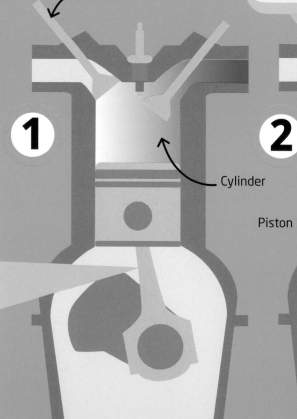

Valve

1

Cylinder

2

Piston

Fuel in

On the first stroke, the piston moves down. It pulls fuel and air into the cylinder through a valve at the top of the piston.

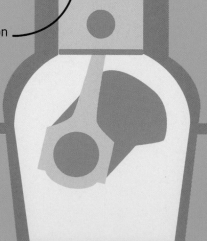

Steam engine These engines are powered by burning coal. The heat of the burning coal turns water into steam, which moves the pistons.

Jet engine Planes have big, powerful engines. They push hot air backward to move the plane forward.

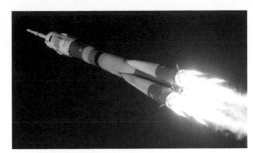

Rocket engine Rockets need extremely powerful engines to launch themselves into space. They use huge amounts of fuel.

Spark

On the third stroke, the spark plug makes a spark, so that the fuel catches fire. The burning fuel spreads out, which pushes the piston down.

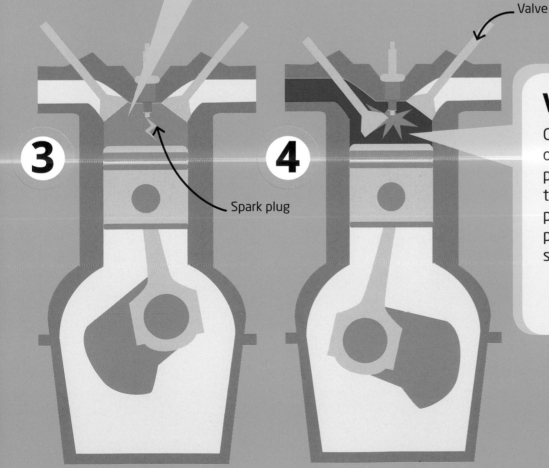

Valve

3

Spark plug

4

Waste out

On the last stroke, the other valve opens. The piston moves up, and the waste products are pushed out. The waste products are carbon dioxide, steam, and pollution.

Robot arm

Robots are machines that can do all kinds of things. Many robots are complicated—they are made up of lots of small parts and computers that make them work. This experiment shows you how to make a simple robot arm that you can use to pick things up.

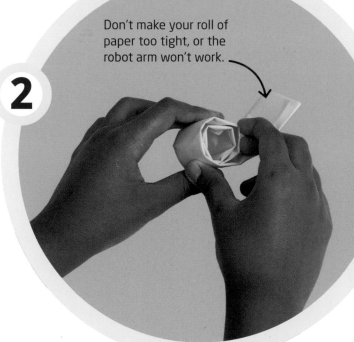

Don't make your roll of paper too tight, or the robot arm won't work.

2

Starting at one end, roll up your strip of paper like a snail shell. You'll need to hold it to keep the paper from coming unrolled.

Fold your paper up to make a long strip.

1

Fold a piece of paper over and over itself lengthwise until it makes a strip about 1½ in (4 cm) wide.

Put one rubber band near the end farthest from the paper.

Put the other rubber band where the paper roll is.

3

Place the rolled-up paper between the two rulers, about 1½ in (4 cm) from one end. Wrap two rubber bands around the rulers—one where the paper roll is and the other toward the opposite end.

What can you pick up?

4

Press the ends of the rulers together to "open" the robot arm. When you let go, the rulers will close, and you can pick things up.

Factory robots

Robot arms are used in factories. In addition to picking things up, they can move things around or put them together. Robots do the same thing over and over again, very fast and without making mistakes.

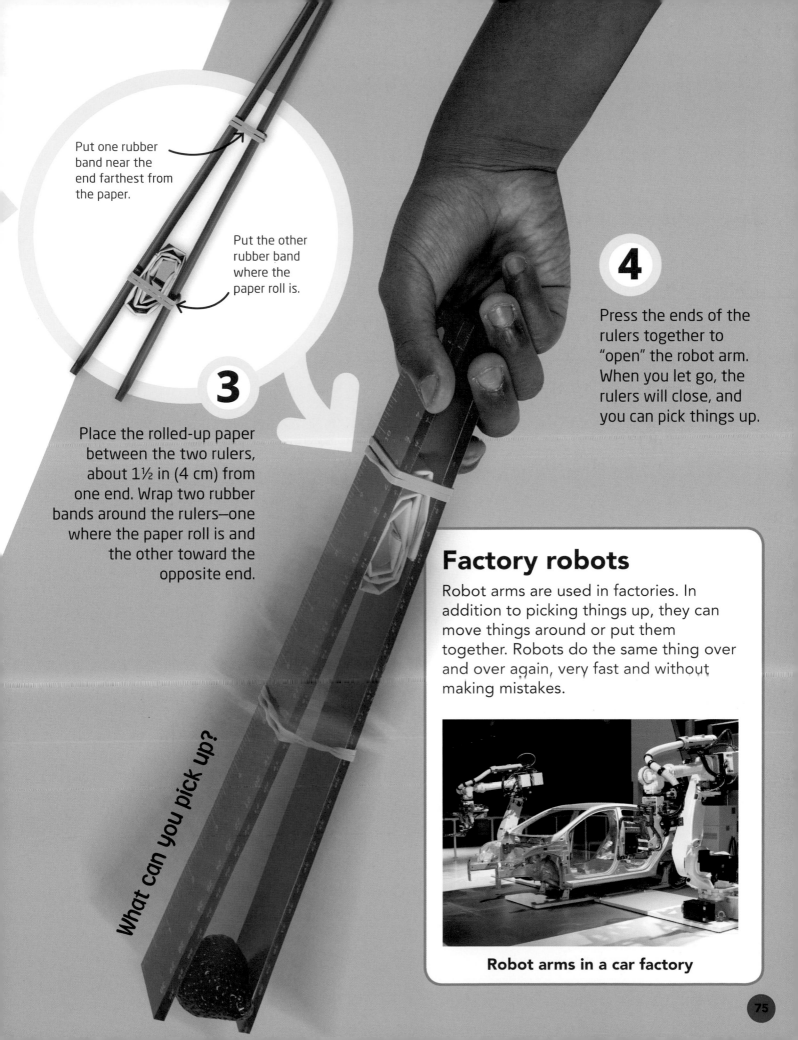

Robot arms in a car factory

Robots

Robots are machines that follow instructions. They help us do a range of things, from simple daily chores to complicated and sometimes even dangerous jobs. Robots may seem intelligent, but even the most advanced ones are only able to follow the instructions humans have given them.

Extreme

Robots can be sent to places that humans can't go because they are dangerous or unknown: for example, deep underground or to other planets. The *Curiosity* rover has been sending us information about the planet Mars since 2011.

Humanoid

Humanoid robots are modeled to look and move like humans. They can walk, talk, and do simple tasks. Some even react to our feelings and the expressions on our faces.

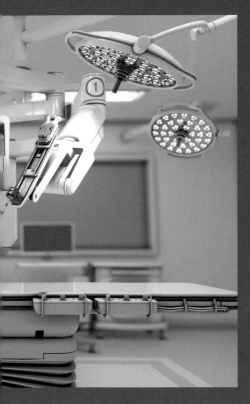

This robot dog is designed to act like a real pet.

Medical

Operations need to be very precise. Medical robots help doctors with complicated surgery because they are more steady and reliable than humans.

The robot dog is capable of playing with other toys, such as balls.

Entertainment

Robotic toys are fun. They are designed to play games or respond to people. Robot toys are usually made to look cute—for example, like a pet.

Robotic vacuum cleaners clean floors without requiring a person to push them around.

Domestic

These robots carry out household chores. Many of them are very simple. Engineers are developing more robot household help, such as a refrigerator that can bring you drinks.

Factory

Robots in factories do the same things over and over again, very fast. They help make food, clothes, and cars.

Factory robots can make things much faster than people can.

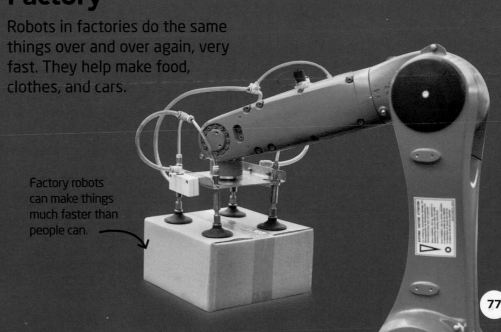

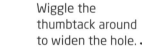

Cup phones

Sound travels in waves through the air. Did you know that sound can also travel through other things? Engineers use various materials, called mediums, to control how sound travels. In this experiment, you will use the medium of string!

Wiggle the thumbtack around to widen the hole.

Talk into the cup to give a message.

Make sure the string is tight.

First phones

In 1876, Alexander Graham Bell engineered a device that changed sound waves into electrical patterns. These patterns were sent through wires before being turned back into sound waves. This device became known as the telephone.

An early telephone designed by Alexander Graham Bell

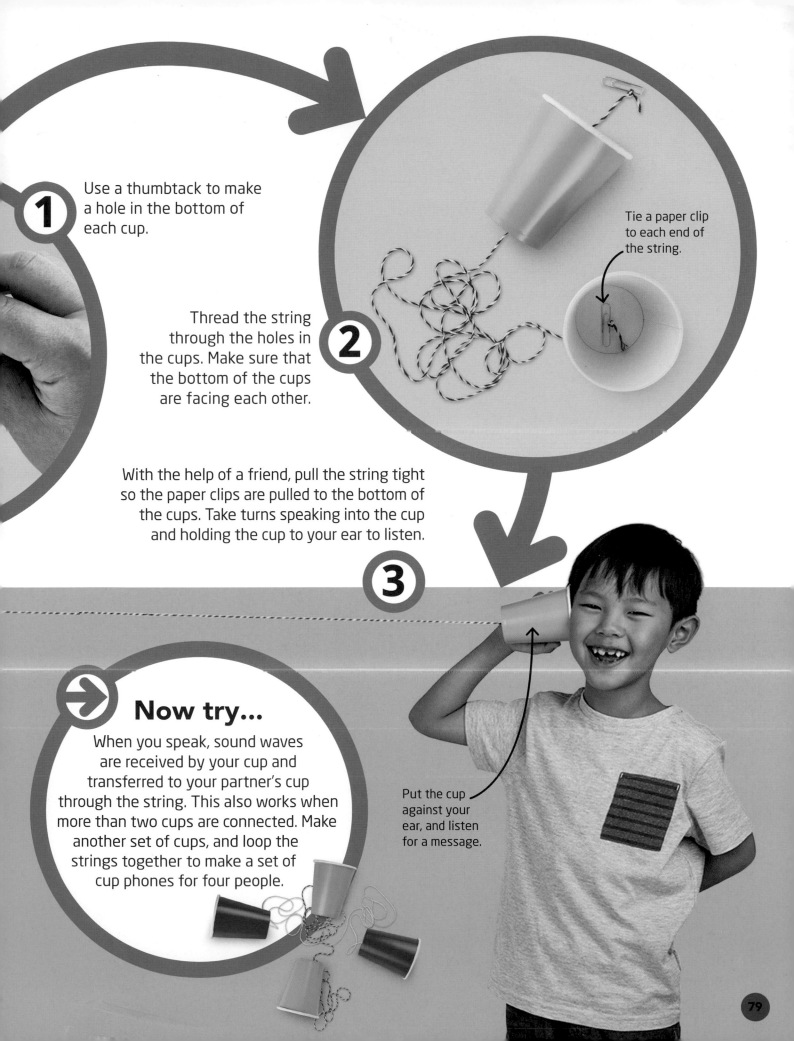

1 Use a thumbtack to make a hole in the bottom of each cup.

2 Thread the string through the holes in the cups. Make sure that the bottom of the cups are facing each other.

Tie a paper clip to each end of the string.

3 With the help of a friend, pull the string tight so the paper clips are pulled to the bottom of the cups. Take turns speaking into the cup and holding the cup to your ear to listen.

Put the cup against your ear, and listen for a message.

→ Now try...

When you speak, sound waves are received by your cup and transferred to your partner's cup through the string. This also works when more than two cups are connected. Make another set of cups, and loop the strings together to make a set of cup phones for four people.

Computers

A computer is a machine. It stores instructions called programs that let it carry out tasks. Computers are all around us—they control traffic lights, let us play video games, and even help pilots fly planes.

Computer words

Some computer-related words might sound complicated. Here they are explained simply.

Hardware
The physical parts of the computer are called its hardware.

Software
Software is the instructions inside the computer that tell it what to do.

Input
The input is how someone tells a computer what to do—for example, by using a mouse.

Looking inside

A computer is made of lots of different parts that all work together.

The processor does the calculations that make the computer work.

The screen is where words and images are shown to the person using the computer.

Types of computer

Computers come in all shapes and sizes. Some computers are enormous, while others are small enough to fit in our pockets.

Supercomputer Huge, powerful computers that perform very complicated tasks are called supercomputers. They are usually used for scientific research.

Supercomputer in action

Minicomputer The Raspberry Pi is a minicomputer that helps teach people the basics of computer science.

The Raspberry Pi is a very simple computer.

Microcomputer Smartphones, tablets, and laptops are microcomputers. They are used by millions of people all over the world.

Smartphones are pocket-size, making them easy to carry around.

The motherboard connects all the parts of the computer together.

The RAM saves information, but only when the computer is turned on.

The hard drive stores data even when the computer is turned off.

Grace Hopper

Pioneer of computer programming
• Born 1906 • From the United States

Grace Hopper was a computer programmer who worked on some of the earliest computers. She invented a way of making it easier to program, or give instructions to, computers. She also had a long career in the US Navy. She was nicknamed "Amazing Grace" because of her achievements.

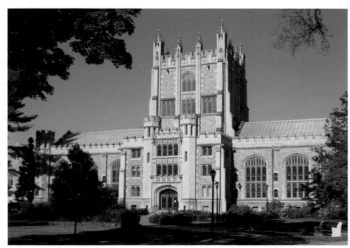

Vassar College

Brilliant mathematician

Hopper had a natural gift for mathematics. She studied it at college and went on to become a mathematics professor at Vassar College in New York State before joining the US Navy.

Rear admiral

Hopper's great-grandfather had been an admiral in the US Navy during the Civil War. Hopper wanted very much to follow in his footsteps. Her chance came in 1943, during World War II, when she joined the US Navy Reserve. She eventually rose to the senior rank of rear admiral.

Early computers

When Hopper joined the navy, she was sent to Harvard College in Massachusetts. There, she worked on programming an early computer, called the Harvard Mark 1. After the war, Hopper helped develop another ground-breaking computer, called the UNIVAC 1.

UNIVAC 1

Compiler

Programming early computers took a huge amount of work. The computers were the size of rooms and very complicated. Hopper figured out a way to make it easier. She developed something called a compiler, which translates words into instructions using numbers and symbols that the computer can understand.

Grace Hopper with a compiler

Debugging

Finding and removing errors, or "bugs," in a computer or a computer program is called debugging. Hopper and her coworkers once had to do some real debugging when they found out that their computer wasn't working because a moth was trapped inside it!

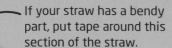
If your straw has a bendy part, put tape around this section of the straw.

Pinch the end of the straw, and push it inside the other to join the straws together.

Use tape to attach the short straw 1½ in (4 cm) from one end of the long straws.

1 Stick two straws together by fitting their ends inside each other. Then do the same thing with another pair of straws. Now, stick the two longer straws together by taping a 2 in (5 cm) piece of straw between them. Now you have an H-shaped structure. Make another nine of these.

Ping-pong
roller coaster

Roller coasters are the result of very clever engineering. They use different types of energy to create maximum speed and fun! Design and build your own ride to send a ping-pong ball zooming through the air.

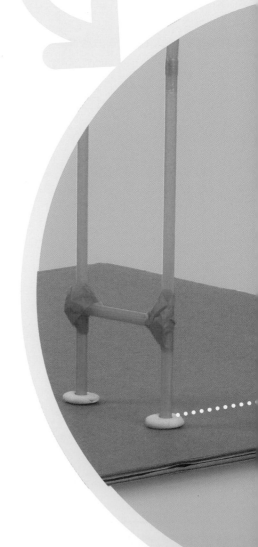

3

Now, create your first crossbeam by putting a small piece of straw across the top of the first tower, securing it with tape. Then, attach another piece of straw to the second tower, slightly lower down than the first.

Make sure the first crossbeam is slightly higher up than the second.

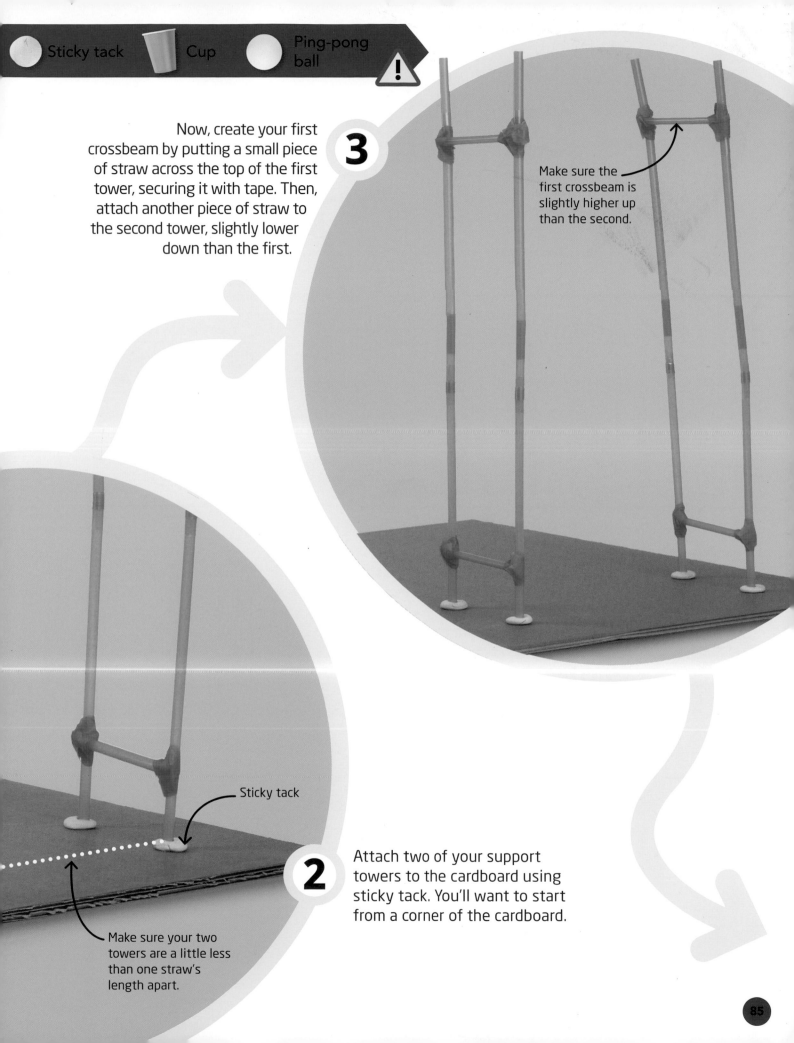

Sticky tack

2 Attach two of your support towers to the cardboard using sticky tack. You'll want to start from a corner of the cardboard.

Make sure your two towers are a little less than one straw's length apart.

Put two straws between the crossbeams of the towers, securing them with tape. You have now made your first section of track.

4

Don't let the track touch the sides of the towers, or your ball might get stuck.

Use the ping-pong ball to check how far apart the straws are. You don't want it to fall through the gap!

Now construction can really start! Add more towers, making a continuous track for your ball to follow.

Add some extra straws to keep the ball from falling off the sides of the track.

5

Each new section should be slightly lower than the last.

Put a cup at the end of the last piece of track, to catch the ball.

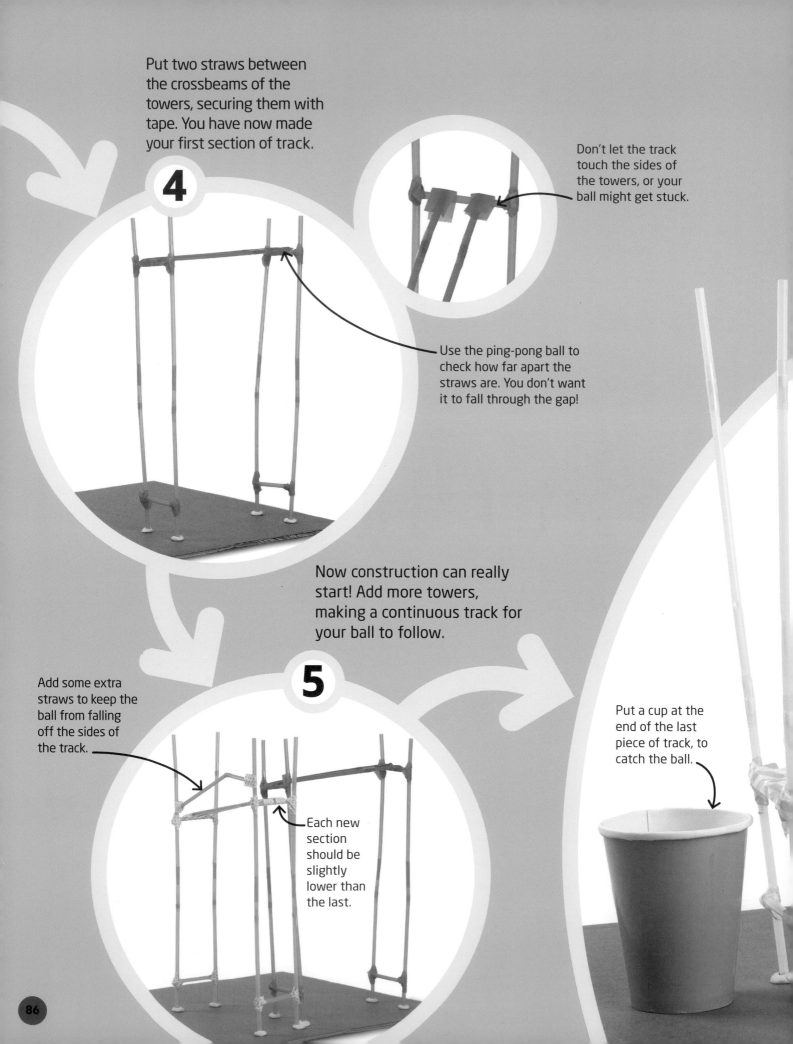

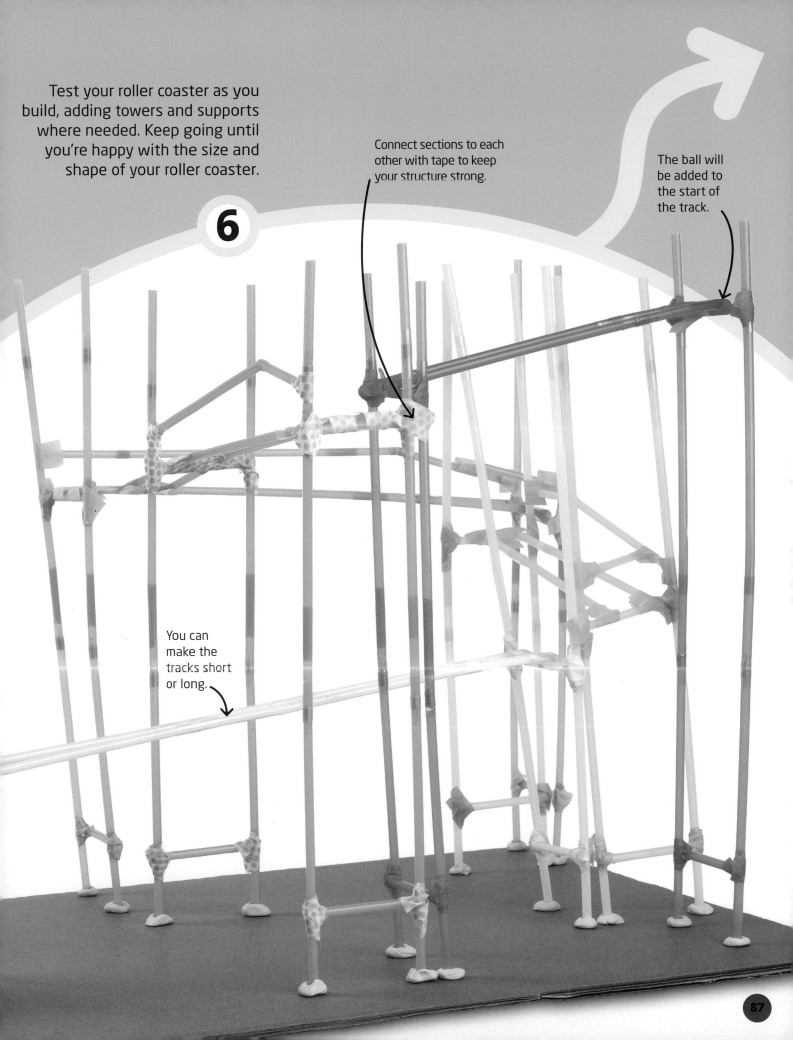

Test your roller coaster as you build, adding towers and supports where needed. Keep going until you're happy with the size and shape of your roller coaster.

6

Connect sections to each other with tape to keep your structure strong.

The ball will be added to the start of the track.

You can make the tracks short or long.

Fun forces

Roller coasters use electricity to power the car up the first hill. As the car slowly climbs up the track, it gains potential, or stored, energy. As it speeds down the hill, the potential energy turns into movement energy.

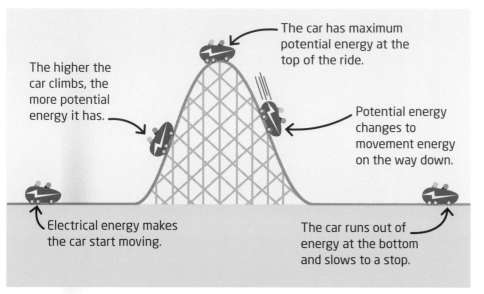

The car has maximum potential energy at the top of the ride.

The higher the car climbs, the more potential energy it has.

Potential energy changes to movement energy on the way down.

Electrical energy makes the car start moving.

The car runs out of energy at the bottom and slows to a stop.

Types of energy that power a roller coaster

7 Your ping-pong roller coaster is ready! Drop your ball, and watch it follow the track. Do you need to make any changes to make your coaster work better?

Now try...

Add more towers and track sections to increase the length of your roller coaster. Can you think of any other features you could add to improve it?

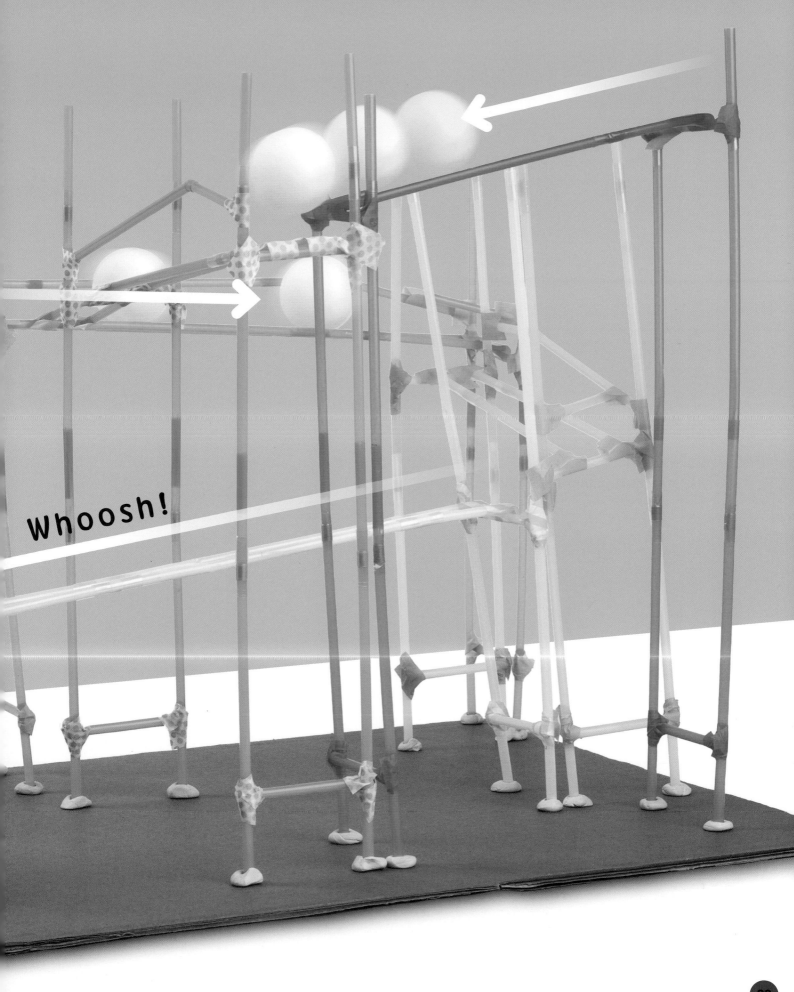

Whoosh!

Helicopters

Boats

Rockets

Bicycles

Buses

Getting around

Planes, trains, and boats are just a few of the many ways that engineers have developed to help us get around. Transportation is constantly improving, letting us travel from one location to another faster than ever before.

Cars

Trains

Shuttles

Airplanes

Hovercrafts

Transportation

Walking is a great way to travel from one place to another, but what if you need to get somewhere faster? Engineers have designed different types of transportation to help us move on land, on water, and in the air. Over time, engineers have improved them so they work better and go even quicker!

Bicycles

The first bicycle was invented around the year 1817. Bicycles are ridden by people and powered by their feet moving up and down on the pedals. This turns a chain, which turns the wheels.

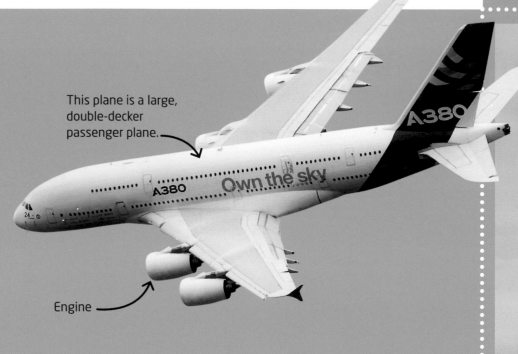

This plane is a large, double-decker passenger plane.

Engine

Airplanes

The first airplane flew through the sky in 1903. Since then, planes have become huge and can fly long distances. They fly very fast, carrying billions of people around the world every year.

This cargo ship carries lots of heavy containers.

Helicopters

Spinning blades called rotors lift helicopters into the air. Helicopters usually fly short distances. Unlike planes, they can go up, down, backward, and sideways.

Rotor

Tail

Trains

Trains move along steel rails called tracks. The first trains were powered by steam, but modern trains use diesel, electricity, or even magnets. They are a fast way for people to travel and for goods to be transported.

Tracks

Ships

Boats and ships help people cross rivers and oceans. Ships are much bigger than boats and can be used to carry heavy loads around the world. Most ships have engines while boats are often pushed along by the wind in their sails.

Cars

The first car was made more than 120 years ago and could only go 6 mph (10 kph). Modern cars are much faster and come in all shapes and sizes. Cars have engines to make them go. Most car engines are powered by fuel, such as gasoline and diesel, but some run on electricity.

Three plastic bendy straws   Scissors   Tape   Ruler

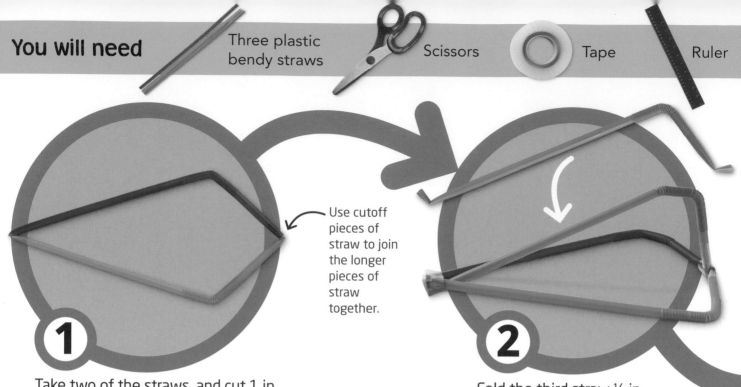

Use cutoff pieces of straw to join the longer pieces of straw together.

1 Take two of the straws, and cut 1 in (2.5 cm) off the long ends. Fold the cutoff pieces in half, and poke them into the ends of the straws to fasten them together. You should now have a diamond shape.

2 Fold the third straw ½ in (1 cm) from each end. Then tape the third straw to the other two to make the bottom of the boat.

Staying afloat

Engineers who design ships use their knowledge of liquids, structures, materials, and more to build boats that float. In this experiment, you will build your own boat. Try to design it so that it can carry as much weight as possible!

 Aluminum foil

 A large container

 Marbles

3

Use a single piece of foil to cover your straw frame. Fold the foil over the edges. This is your boat's hull.

Sinking and floating

Ships don't sink because of something called buoyancy. A buoyant force pushes up on a boat, while the force of gravity pushes it down. When the two forces are equal, the boat floats. If more weight is added to a boat, it increases the force of gravity, and the boat moves down in the water. If weight is added to the point that the force of gravity is greater than the buoyant force, the boat will sink.

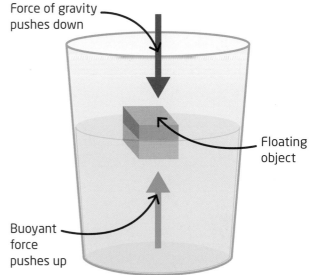

Force of gravity pushes down

Floating object

Buoyant force pushes up

4

Fill your container with water, and launch your boat. Does it float? If so, add marbles into it one by one.

How many marbles can your boat hold before it sinks?

You will need

Two pencils Small plastic container — Three rubber bands

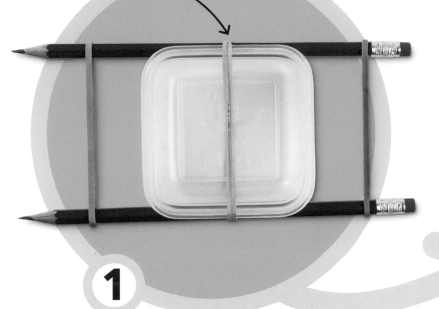

You may need to wrap the bands around twice, to keep everything firmly in place.

You will need two of these. Cut a slit halfway through each.

Slide the two slits into each other.

1

Take two pencils and a small, square plastic container. Use rubber bands to hold the container between the pencils, as shown.

2

Now, cut out two cardboard rectangles the same width as the plastic container. These will be your paddles.

Paddleboat

Powered by steam or pedals, this simple type of boat uses paddles to move. You can test paddle power for yourself in this experiment— make a boat to try out in your bath!

Scissors

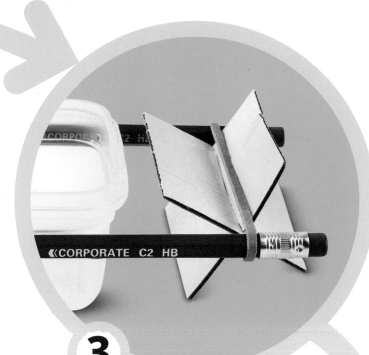

3

Fit the paddles into the rubber band at the back of the boat.

Paddle power

The boat is pushed through the water by movement energy. When you wind up the paddles, you are storing potential energy in the rubber band. That potential energy is released as movement energy when the paddles hit the water, and the boat moves forward.

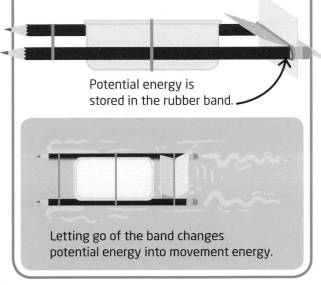

Potential energy is stored in the rubber band.

Letting go of the band changes potential energy into movement energy.

4

Twist the paddles until the rubber band is tight. Place the boat in a sink or bath filled with water. Let go and watch your boat go!

Robert Stephenson

Railroad and civil engineer
- Born in 1803 • From Britain

Robert Stephenson is best remembered for his steam locomotive *Rocket*, which he built in 1829. Its modern design was copied for 150 years. He also built many of Britain's earliest railroads, as well as new types of bridges that are still in use today.

The chimney lets out steam and smoke.

In his father's footsteps

Robert's father, George, was also an engineer. Robert and his father built the world's first public railroad. It opened in 1825 and ran for 27 miles (43 km). Later, they built the first railroad between Liverpool and Manchester.

The opening of the first public railroad

Rocket man

Robert and his father also designed steam engines. They entered their designs into the Rainhill Trials in 1829, where Robert's design, a locomotive called *Rocket*, was the clear winner. It reached a top speed of about 30 mph (48 kph).

Railroads

Railroads were very important in Britain in the 1830s. Robert was the chief engineer on many lines, including the London and Birmingham Railway. His work involved studying the countryside to figure out the best routes and blasting tunnels through hills.

Robert Stephenson was great friends with **another famous engineer, Isambard Kingdom Brunel.**

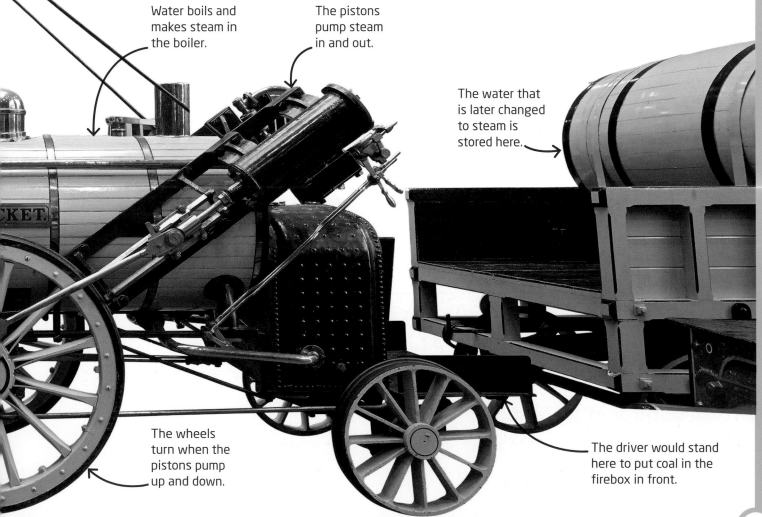

Water boils and makes steam in the boiler.

The pistons pump steam in and out.

The water that is later changed to steam is stored here.

The wheels turn when the pistons pump up and down.

The driver would stand here to put coal in the firebox in front.

Get an adult to add hot, but not boiling, water to the bowl, until it reaches the same level as the water in the bottle.

2

Ask an adult to help with the hot water.

1

Pour about 2 in (5 cm) of water into the bottle. Place the bottle in a bowl. Stuff the balloon inside the bottle, and stretch the balloon neck around the bottle opening.

Steam power

Steam rises, which means it can be used to move things. It has been used to power ships, trains, and factory machines. Steam power is still used to produce over 80 percent of the world's electricity. This experiment shows how you can use steam power to lift objects.

Steam power should push the cardboard off the bottle.

Does the steam in your bottle have enough power to lift the cardboard?

2. The steam moves mechanical parts called pistons back and forth.

1. Fire heats the water, creating steam.

3. The movement of the pistons makes the wheels turn.

Age of steam

Steam locomotives use fire to heat water and make steam. This steam moves pistons up and down, which then turns the wheels of the train. The first moving steam engine was invented in 1829.

3 Carefully put the piece of cardboard on top of the bottle. The heat from the bowl of water will make the air inside the bottle expand, pushing the balloon up and the cardboard off.

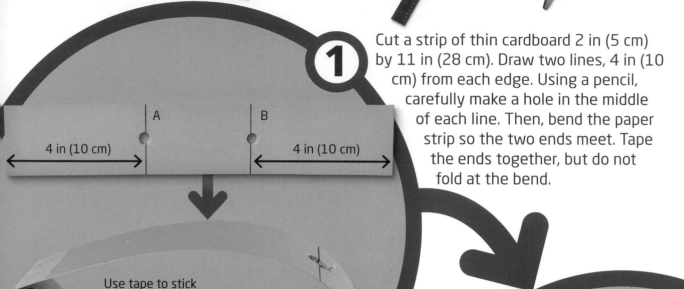

1 Cut a strip of thin cardboard 2 in (5 cm) by 11 in (28 cm). Draw two lines, 4 in (10 cm) from each edge. Using a pencil, carefully make a hole in the middle of each line. Then, bend the paper strip so the two ends meet. Tape the ends together, but do not fold at the bend.

A   B

4 in (10 cm)   4 in (10 cm)

Use tape to stick the ends together.

Make sure your skewer points straight up from the ground.

Wings for flying

If you've ever wondered how planes stay in the air, this is the experiment for you! Plane wings use forces that normally pin us to the ground. With the right shape, you can make an airfoil, or wing, that uses air pressure to lift it up.

2 Stick the end of your wooden skewer into a ball of sticky tack. Stick the tack to a flat surface. You now have a testing rig for your wing. Next, slide the wing onto the skewer through the holes. Put a marble-sized ball of sticky tack on top of the skewer.

Tape   Sticky tack   Wooden skewer   Hair dryer   ⚠

Turn on the hair dryer. Hold it in front of the bend in the wing **③** with slightly more air flowing over the top of the wing. Change the position of the hair dryer slightly until the wing "flies" up the skewer.

Winging it

The shape of a plane's wing makes air flow faster over the top than the bottom. Faster-flowing air has lower pressure than slower air. This means that the air moving over the top of the wing has lower pressure than the slower-moving air under it. This difference in pressure makes the wing move toward the low pressure zone, creating lift.

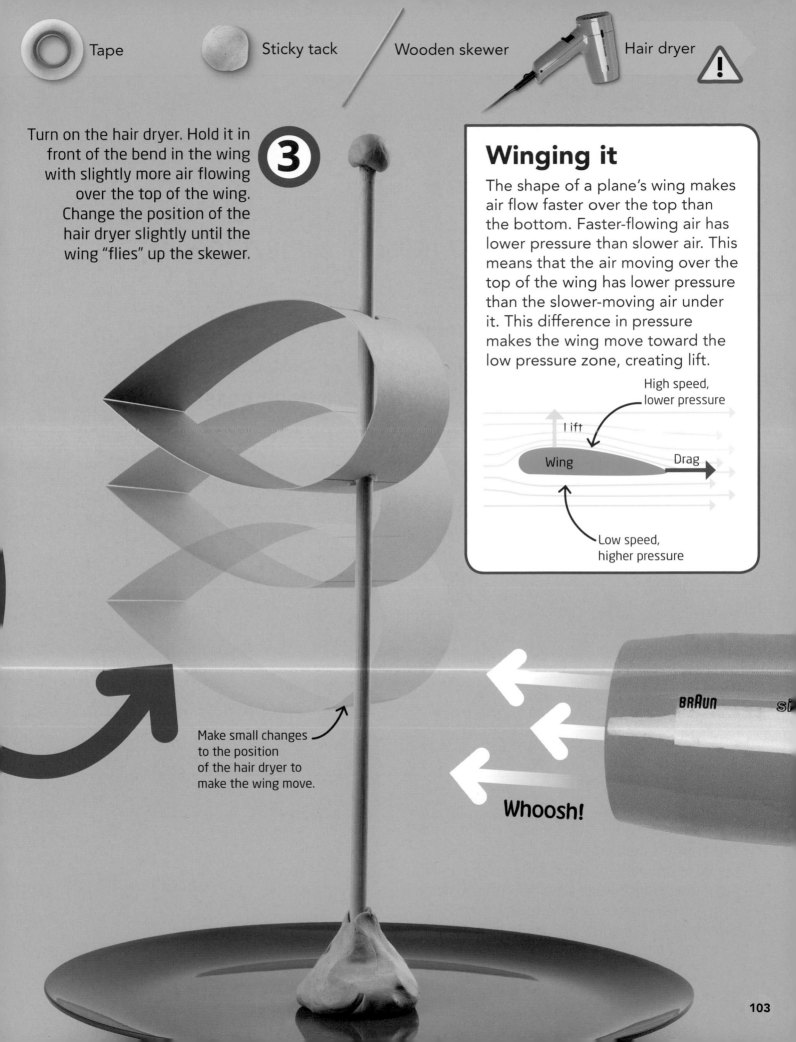

High speed, lower pressure

Lift

Wing

Drag

Low speed, higher pressure

Make small changes to the position of the hair dryer to make the wing move.

BRAUN   si

Whoosh!

Wright brothers

Engineers • Born in 1867 (Wilbur) and 1871 (Orville) • From the United States

When we want to travel somewhere far away, we take it for granted that we can get on an airplane and get there in hours. This would never have been possible without Wilbur and Orville Wright, who invented the powered plane.

These flaps made the plane go up and down.

Early Life

Wilbur and Orville Wright were brothers who grew up in Dayton, Ohio. They became interested in flying when their father bought them a flying toy. As young men, they bought and repaired bicycles.

Gliders

The brothers studied birds to figure out how the different parts of their wings moved during flight. They made huge kites and then gliders with narrow wings. Part of the wings was controlled by the pilot, who could then steer the glider.

Wilbur Wright in a glider

The *Wright Flyer*

When the brothers were happy with their glider, they added an engine and two propellers to power the plane. They called their plane the *Wright Flyer I*. The first flight took place in 1903. It lasted for 12 seconds and covered 120 ft (37 m). This was the first-ever powered flight—the Wright brothers had made history!

The first flight of the *Wright Flyer I*

The wings on the *Wright Flyer I* were about 40 ft (12 m) long.

The propellers drove the plane and were behind the pilot.

The rudder at the back turned the aircraft right or left.

The pilot would lie on his stomach next to the engine.

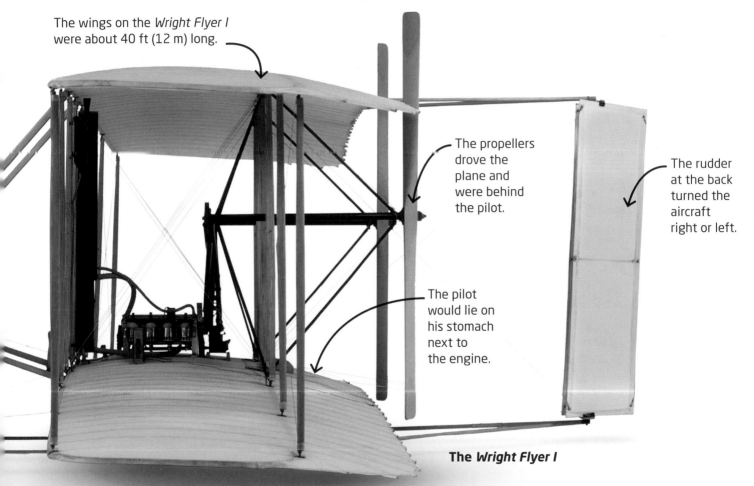

The *Wright Flyer I*

Modern airplanes

The *Wright Flyer I* made the brothers and their company, the Wright Company, celebrities. They continued to build more planes, which influenced later ideas such as the jet engine and modern-day planes.

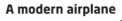

A modern airplane

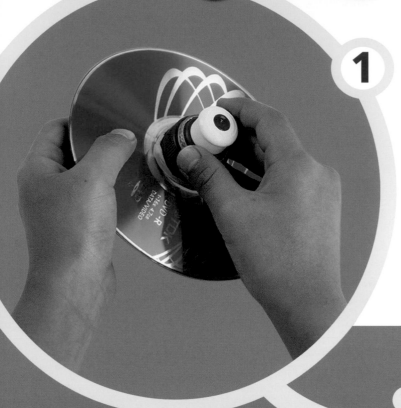

1 Use sticky tack to attach the bottle cap to the CD. Make sure the seal between the CD and the bottle cap is airtight. Pull the cap to the open position.

Twist the neck of the balloon several times to keep air from escaping.

You will need only a short section of cardboard tube.

2

Balloon hovercraft

Hovercrafts hover using a special cushion of air between themselves and the ground or water underneath. They move best over smooth surfaces. Use a balloon and a CD to make your own.

Blow up the balloon, and pull the end through the cardboard tube without letting the air out. Stretch the balloon opening over the cap, and pull it as far down onto the cap as you can. You may need help!

Cardboard
tube

Scissors

⚠

Land and water

Hovercrafts can travel on land and
water. They don't have wheels but
aren't boats either! Instead,
they use powerful fans to pump
air down into a big, rubber skirt.
The air is trapped in the skirt,
making a cushion of air that the
craft travels on.

Hovercraft

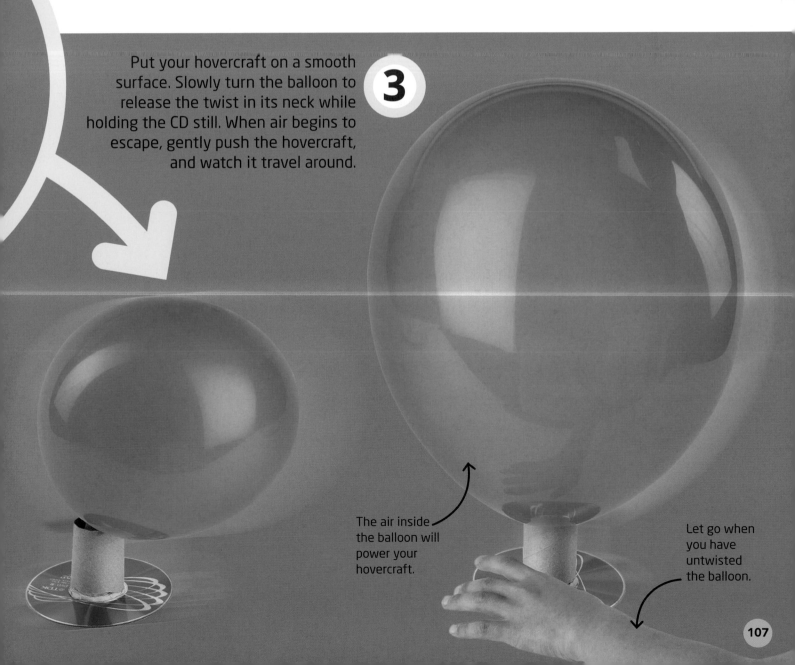

Put your hovercraft on a smooth
surface. Slowly turn the balloon to
release the twist in its neck while
holding the CD still. When air begins to
escape, gently push the hovercraft,
and watch it travel around.

3

The air inside
the balloon will
power your
hovercraft.

Let go when
you have
untwisted
the balloon.

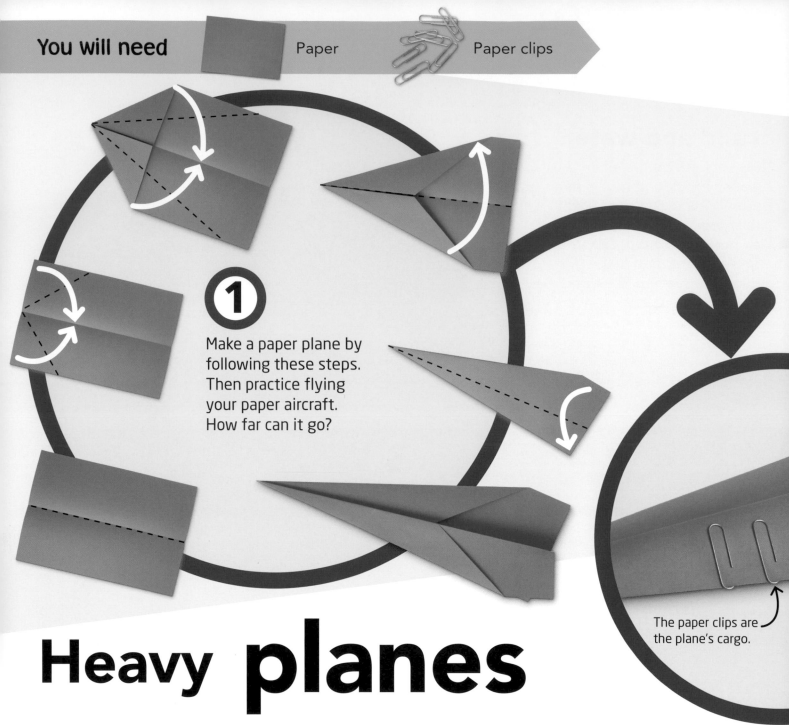

①

Make a paper plane by following these steps. Then practice flying your paper aircraft. How far can it go?

The paper clips are the plane's cargo.

Heavy planes

Have you ever wondered why sports cars are a different shape than buses? Or why sneakers look different from rain boots? They are each designed for a different purpose. Engineers use a process called optimization to create machines and products that are perfect for specific tasks. In this experiment, you will build a paper plane, and then optimize it to carry heavy weights.

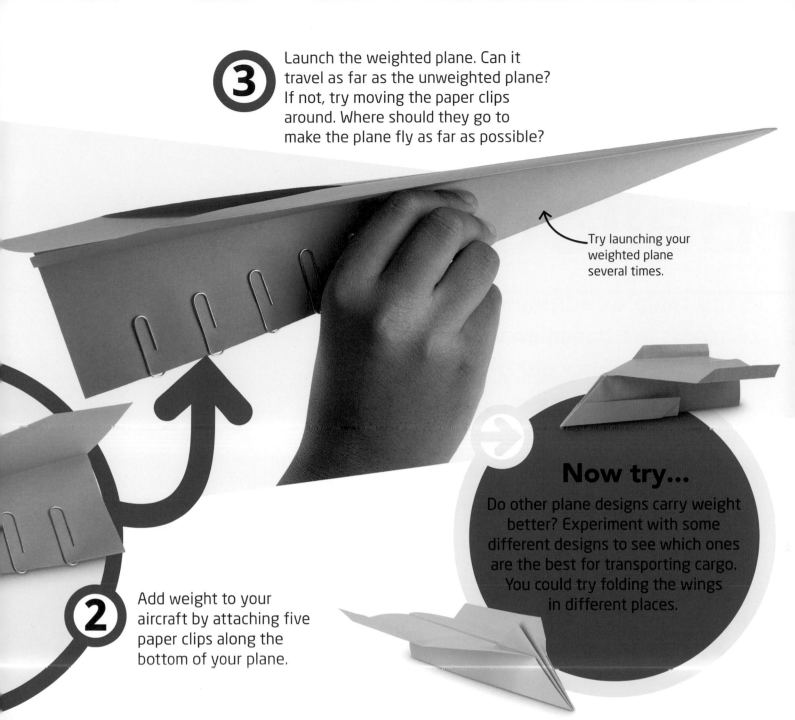

3 Launch the weighted plane. Can it travel as far as the unweighted plane? If not, try moving the paper clips around. Where should they go to make the plane fly as far as possible?

Try launching your weighted plane several times.

2 Add weight to your aircraft by attaching five paper clips along the bottom of your plane.

Now try...

Do other plane designs carry weight better? Experiment with some different designs to see which ones are the best for transporting cargo. You could try folding the wings in different places.

Mega plane

The amazing NASA *Super Guppy* carries parts for rockets, space stations, and other huge machines across the world. It is specially designed to easily load and transport objects that are too big to fit on any other plane.

Jet balloon

Many complex engineering concepts are based on very simple ideas. Air rushing out of something can make that thing move forward. You can see this happen when you let go of a balloon. This same idea is used to make planes, cars, and even rockets go.

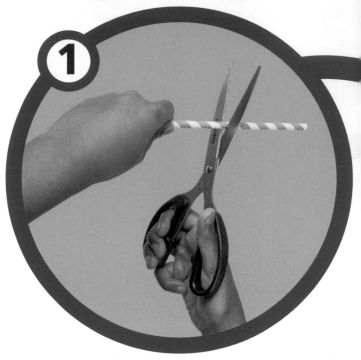

1

Cut your straw in half to make it shorter. Then thread your string through the shortened straw.

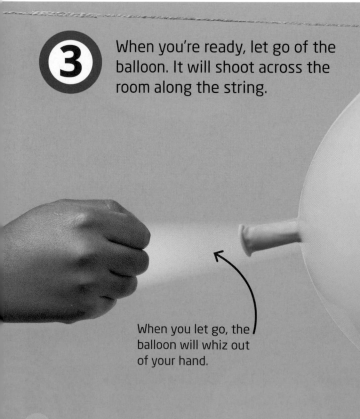

3 When you're ready, let go of the balloon. It will shoot across the room along the string.

When you let go, the balloon will whiz out of your hand.

Now tie each end of the string to a secure object on either side of the room, such as a chair. Blow up your balloon, but use your fingers to keep it shut—don't let go yet! Stick the balloon to the straw.

Use tape to stick the inflated balloon to the straw.

2

Jet engines

Jet engines can make things move extremely fast. They are usually used on planes, such as jumbo jets. To propel themselves, jet engines use air mixed with fuel. The engine takes in air, mixes it with fuel, and burns the mixture to create a gas, which comes out very fast. The engine moves in the opposite direction of the gas, in the same way the balloon moves away from the air coming out of it.

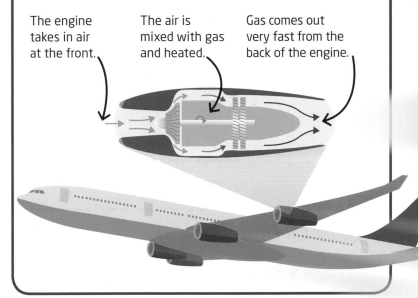

The engine takes in air at the front.

The air is mixed with gas and heated.

Gas comes out very fast from the back of the engine.

Whoooooooosshhhhh! →

Sailboat

When people first added sails to their boats, it let them cross oceans and discover new lands. Follow these easy steps to make a sailboat. You'll see how a sail uses wind power to push the boat forward.

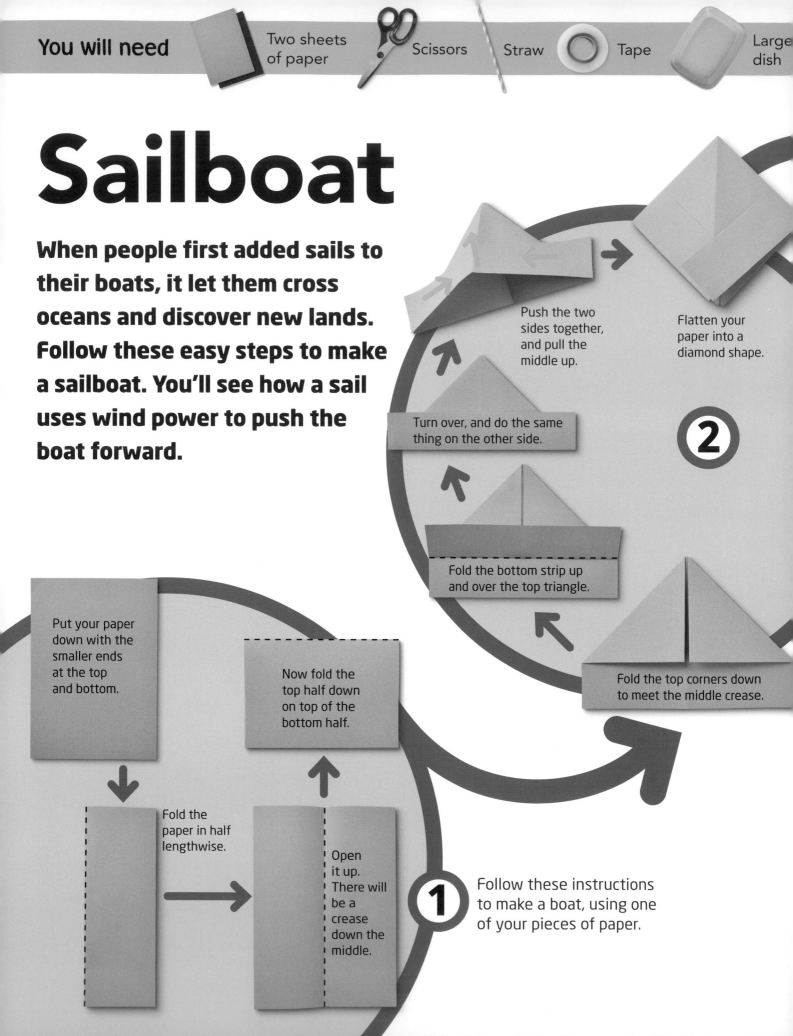

Push the two sides together, and pull the middle up.

Flatten your paper into a diamond shape.

Turn over, and do the same thing on the other side.

②

Fold the bottom strip up and over the top triangle.

Fold the top corners down to meet the middle crease.

Put your paper down with the smaller ends at the top and bottom.

Now fold the top half down on top of the bottom half.

Fold the paper in half lengthwise.

Open it up. There will be a crease down the middle.

① Follow these instructions to make a boat, using one of your pieces of paper.

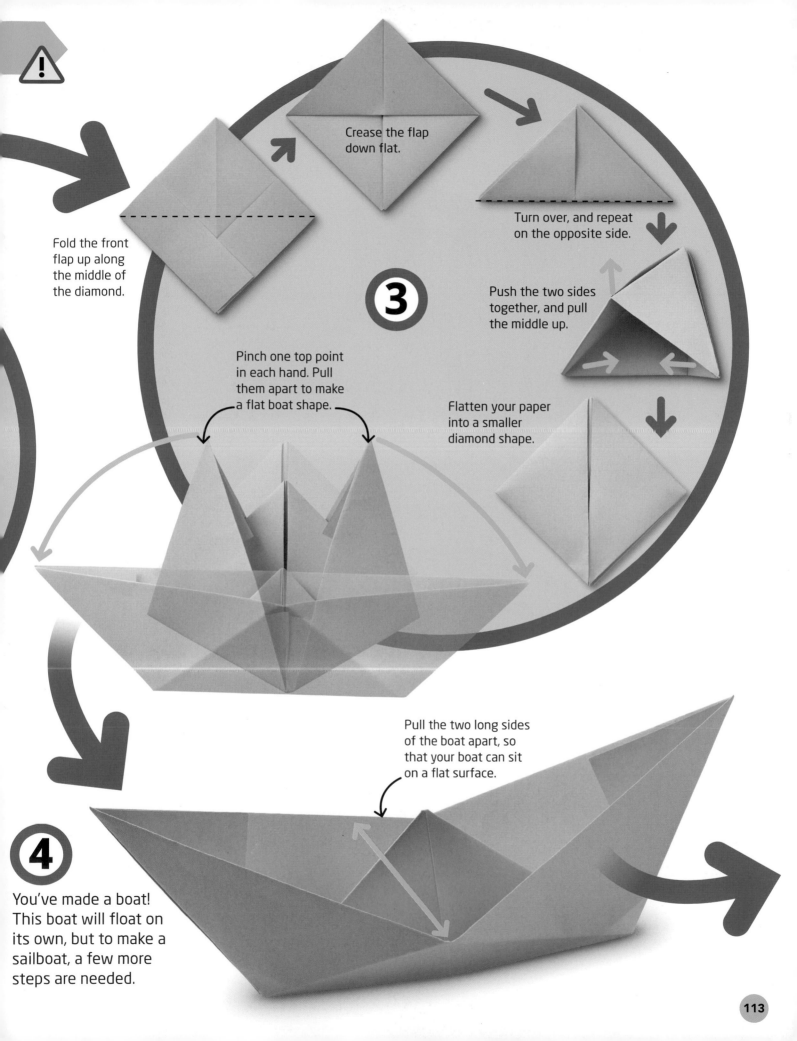

Fold the front flap up along the middle of the diamond.

Crease the flap down flat.

Turn over, and repeat on the opposite side.

Push the two sides together, and pull the middle up.

③

Flatten your paper into a smaller diamond shape.

Pinch one top point in each hand. Pull them apart to make a flat boat shape.

Pull the two long sides of the boat apart, so that your boat can sit on a flat surface.

④

You've made a boat! This boat will float on its own, but to make a sailboat, a few more steps are needed.

Finally, attach the mast and sail to your boat. **7**

Run the straw in and out through the holes in the sail.

6 Put the mast and sail together by pushing a straw through the holes in the paper.

Use tape to attach the mast to the middle of your boat.

Then make two small cuts in the paper for the mast, and then unfold the sail.

5 Next, you need to make a sail for your boat, using the other piece of paper. Use scissors to cut the paper into a triangle.

Make a fold in the long edge of the triangle, a little way in from the edge.

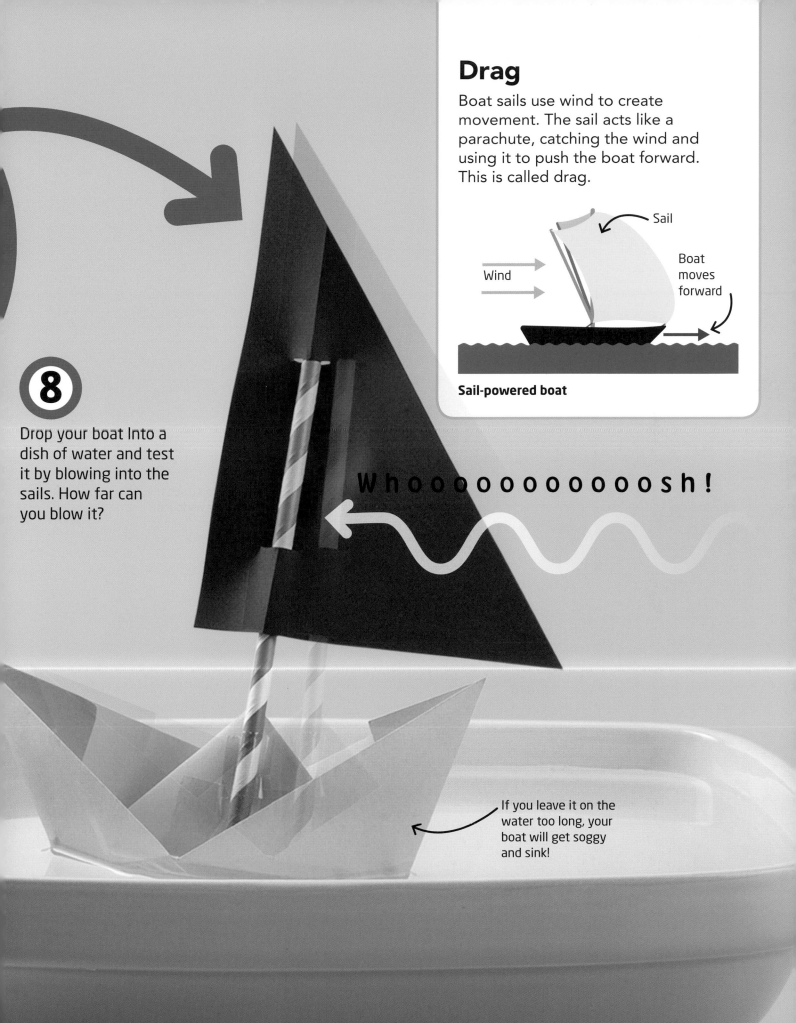

Drag

Boat sails use wind to create movement. The sail acts like a parachute, catching the wind and using it to push the boat forward. This is called drag.

Sail

Wind

Boat moves forward

Sail-powered boat

8

Drop your boat Into a dish of water and test it by blowing into the sails. How far can you blow it?

Whooooooooooosh!

If you leave it on the water too long, your boat will get soggy and sink!

Turbines

Electricity

Generators

Water

Steam

Incredible energy

Energy is what makes things happen. It can be made by burning fossil fuels, or from the power of the sun, wind, or water. Everything we do relies on energy!

Wind

Fuel

Dams

Fossil fuels

Solar power

What is energy?

Energy is what makes things happen. It comes in many forms and is needed for everyday things like walking, making cars go, and lighting homes. Nothing could happen without energy.

Saving energy

Energy is limited, so people try to find ways not to waste it. We use energy to heat our homes. One way to save heat energy is by putting thick layers of material in the roof, which is called insulation. This stops heat from escaping.

In this thermal imaging photo, the red areas are hottest. You can see the roof is colder than the walls, because it has been insulated.

Storing energy

Energy can be stored up for later use. When we eat, food is stored as energy in our bodies for the future. Stored energy is called potential energy.

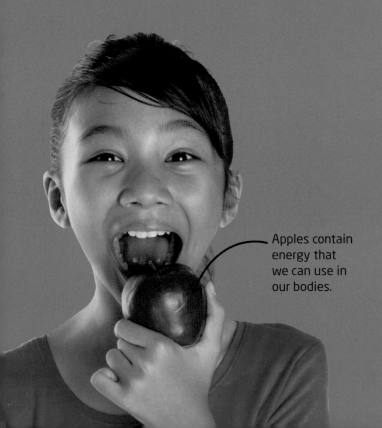

Apples contain energy that we can use in our bodies.

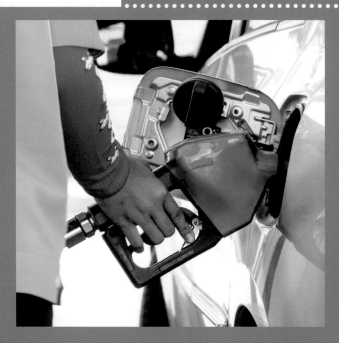

Fossil fuels

There are three types of fossil fuel: coal, gas, and oil. These fuels are made from animals and plants that died millions of years ago, before being buried underground. Fossil fuels are full of energy. We use them to power cars and to cook food.

Changing energy

Energy cannot be created or destroyed, but it can be changed from one type into another. For example, light bulbs change electrical energy into light energy.

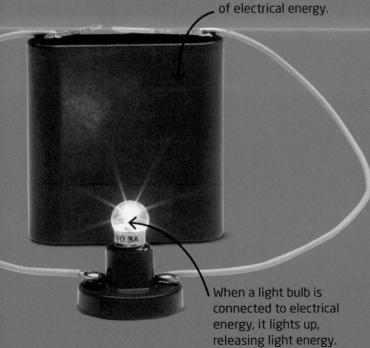

Batteries are sources of electrical energy.

When a light bulb is connected to electrical energy, it lights up, releasing light energy.

Types of energy

There are many types of energy, and energy constantly changes from one type to another.

Movement energy Everything that moves has movement energy. The faster something moves, the more movement energy it has.

Heat energy Hot things have more energy than cold things. The energy of hot things is called heat energy.

Chemical energy Food stores energy in the chemicals inside it. When we eat food, its chemical energy is released.

Nuclear energy This type of energy is released when atoms—the tiny building blocks of matter—are split apart.

Electrical energy Electricity is the flow of tiny charged particles called electrons. We use electricity to power things in our homes.

Sound energy When something moves backward and forward very fast, it sends waves of energy traveling through the air. We hear these waves as sounds.

Light energy Glowing things give off light energy, which we can see. Light bulbs and the sun both release light energy.

Stored energy This is energy stored up in our bodies. You could use your stored energy to dive, run, or jump.

Wind energy

Engineers have figured out how to use wind to make energy. Use the power of wind for yourself by making your own windmill.

Use a thumbtack secure your windmill to the sticky tack.

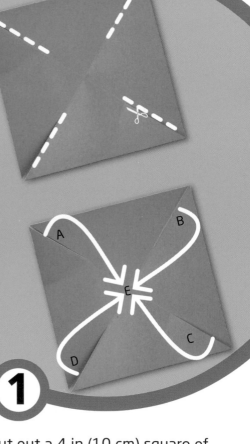

1 Cut out a 4 in (10 cm) square of thin cardboard. Make a cut from each corner to about halfway to the center. Fold each corner into the middle, and glue it in place. You've made a windmill!

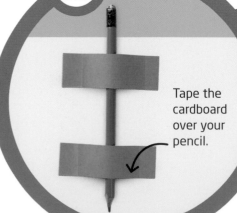

2 Tape the cardboard over your pencil.

Cut out two cardboard rectangles, and tape them over the pencil, securing it to the work surface. The end of the pencil needs to hang over the edge.

Tie the button to the other end of the string.

3 Place a blob of tack on the end of the pencil. Attach your windmill to it by pushing the thumbtack through the cardboard and into the tack. Then, tape one end of the string onto the pencil.

4 Try blowing on your windmill to make it spin. The pencil should start winding up the string.

As the string wraps around the pencil, wind energy makes the button move up.

Wind power

Wind turbines are used to turn wind energy into electricity we can use. A group of many wind turbines is called a wind farm. They can be spread over hundreds of miles.

Nikola Tesla

Electrical engineer and inventor
• Born 1856 • From present-day Croatia

Nikola Tesla had a photographic memory that was so good he could design his inventions in his mind. He is most famous for his work with alternating current (AC) electricity. This is the way electricity is transmitted throughout the world.

Early discoveries

While Tesla was working as an electrician at a telephone company, he discovered that electric machines work better when the flow of electricity moves back and forth. Using this alternating current, he created the induction motor, which uses a spinning magnet to create movement.

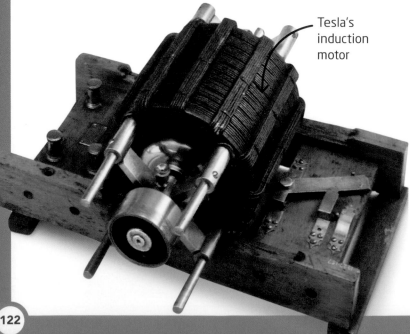

Tesla's induction motor

Tesla coil

In 1891, Tesla invented the Tesla coil, a machine that makes lightning bolts. He used this machine to make the first neon lights, X-ray photographs, and to move energy from place to place without using wires.

Physicists measure the strength of magnetic fields in a unit called the Tesla.

So many ideas

During his lifetime, Tesla came up with hundreds of ideas. The inventions included a radio-controlled boat and an earthquake machine. His ideas helped develop radio, air travel, and radar, which helps planes avoid flying into each other.

Engraving showing Tesla's coil creating lightning bolts

Electricity

Electricity is a type of energy. It is the flow of tiny charged particles called electrons. Many things around us depend on electricity to work—without it we wouldn't be able to light up a dark room, keep food in a refrigerator, or wash our clothes in a machine.

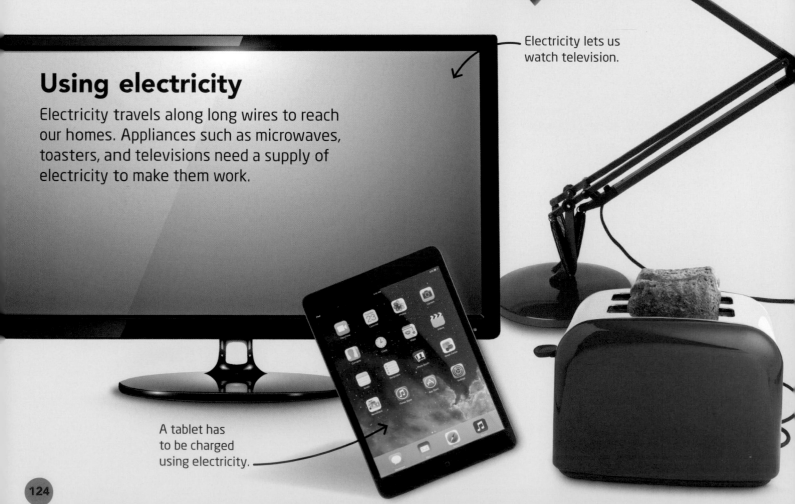

Light bulbs need electricity to shine.

Electricity lets us watch television.

Using electricity

Electricity travels along long wires to reach our homes. Appliances such as microwaves, toasters, and televisions need a supply of electricity to make them work.

A tablet has to be charged using electricity.

Lightning is a spark of static electricity in the sky.

Static electricity

Static electricity happens when electricity builds up in one place. The charge stays still until it finds a way to escape—for example, as lightning.

Rubbing a balloon creates static electricity, making things stick to the balloon.

Making electricity

Electricity is made from other types of energy, such as heat or movement energy. There are two main ways of making electricity—from fossil fuels or from renewable types of energy.

Fossil fuels Most of the world's electricity is made from fossil fuels: coal, oil, and gas. However, the amount of fossil fuels is limited—eventually we will run out of them.

Renewable energy Some types of energy will not run out, such as the movement of wind and water, or the heat of the sun. These are called renewable energy sources.

1 Draw a square 2 in (5 cm) away from the edge of the box lid. Cut along three sides. The other side will be the hinge.

2 Wrap aluminum foil around the flap you made, making sure the shiny side faces out. Open the box lid, and cover the hole with plastic wrap, using tape to keep it in place.

Sun power

The sun is the largest source of energy for earth. More solar energy hits the planet in one day than the whole human race could use in 27 years! With this experiment, you can use the sun's energy to cook a marshmallow.

3 Cover the bottom of the box with black paper.

126

Solar ovens

In areas without electricity, solar ovens can be a great option. They can reach temperatures between 250 and 350 °F (120–175 °C). Solar ovens use the sun's energy to clean water, cook food, and even clean equipment.

4

Put a marshmallow on a cracker inside the box. Place the box in direct sunlight with the flap propped open. Then leave the box for half an hour.

After half an hour, your marshmallow should have begun to melt.

Use a piece of cardboard to prop the flap open.

Make sure sunlight hits the foil and is shining on the marshmallow.

How solar panels work

Solar panels turn energy from the sun into energy that we can use. These panels are put in places with lots of light, such as in big open fields, on rooftops, and on roads.

1 Place the black and white paper next to each other in a sunny spot. Put one ice cube on top of each piece of paper.

Try not to touch the ice cubes too much, or they'll start melting.

The color white reflects light, making the paper cool, so the ice cube melts more slowly.

Sunlight

Dark-colored top layer

Electricity

Inside a solar panel

The top layer of a solar panel is a dark color, to help it absorb energy from the sun. The panel takes this energy and changes it into alternating current (AC) electricity, which we can use to power our homes.

The color black absorbs light from the sun, making the paper hotter, so the ice melts more quickly.

2

Leave the ice cubes for an hour. Which one has melted most?

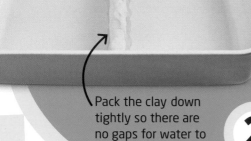

Stick the popsicle sticks to both sides of the clay.

Pack the clay down tightly so there are no gaps for water to get through.

2

Keep adding layers of clay balls until you reach the top of the dish.

3

Add popsicle sticks to both sides of your wall. This will make the wall strong and hold it in place.

Make sure the clay is firmly stuck to the dish.

1

Roll the modeling clay into small balls. Use some of them to make a line down the middle of the dish.

Build a dam

More than 70 percent of the earth is made up of water. Sometimes it can be useful to control this water. Dams are one way of doing this. They let us hold water back in one place until we are ready to let it go.

4

Pour water into one half of the dish.

Giant dam

Three Gorges Dam controls the Yangtze River in China. It is the biggest dam in the world. The dam prevents flooding in areas farther down the river and uses river water to make electricity.

The Three Gorges Dam in China

5

The water should stay on one side of your dish. You've built a dam!

If any water leaks through, try pressing the clay down harder.

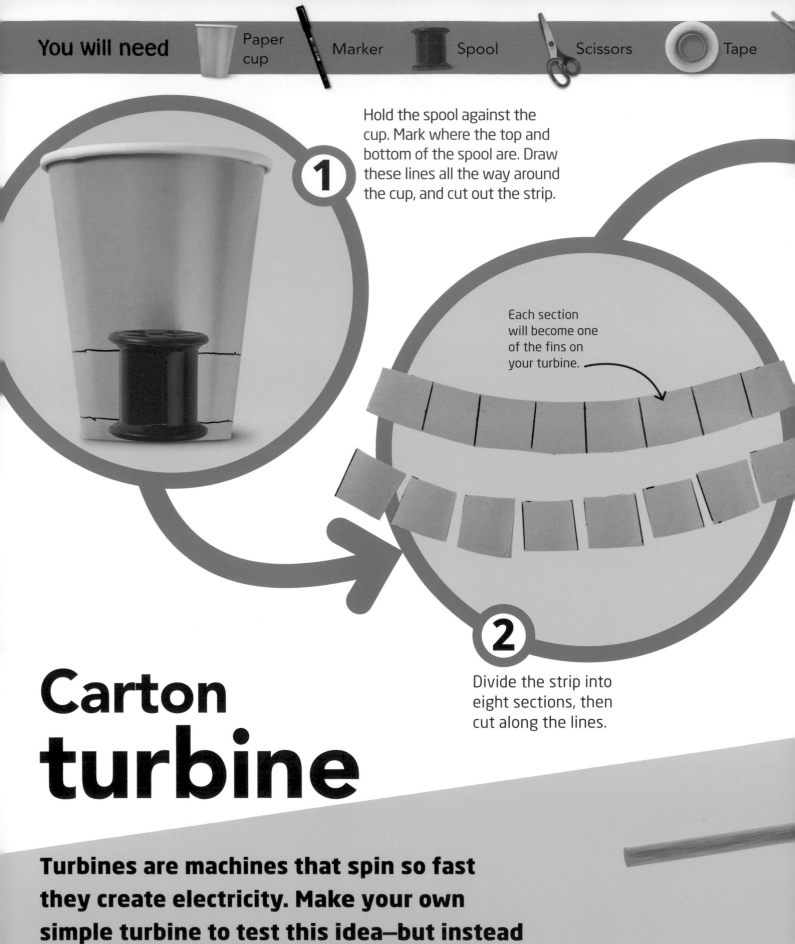

1 Hold the spool against the cup. Mark where the top and bottom of the spool are. Draw these lines all the way around the cup, and cut out the strip.

Each section will become one of the fins on your turbine.

2 Divide the strip into eight sections, then cut along the lines.

Carton turbine

Turbines are machines that spin so fast they create electricity. Make your own simple turbine to test this idea—but instead of making power, you'll be lifting a button.

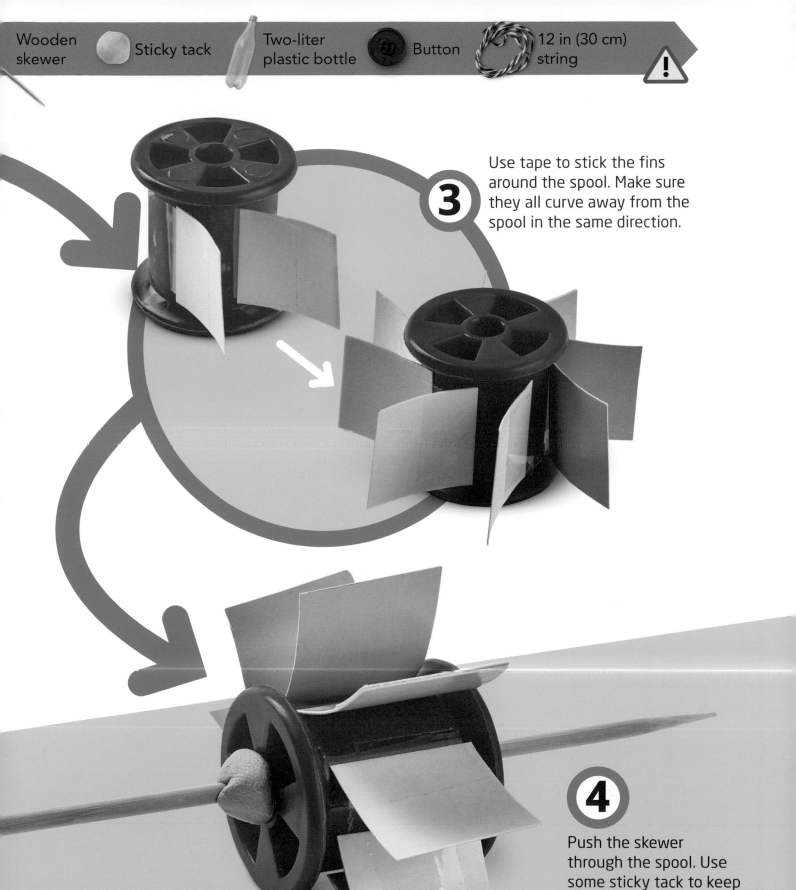

3 Use tape to stick the fins around the spool. Make sure they all curve away from the spool in the same direction.

4 Push the skewer through the spool. Use some sticky tack to keep it in place. This will be the motor of your turbine.

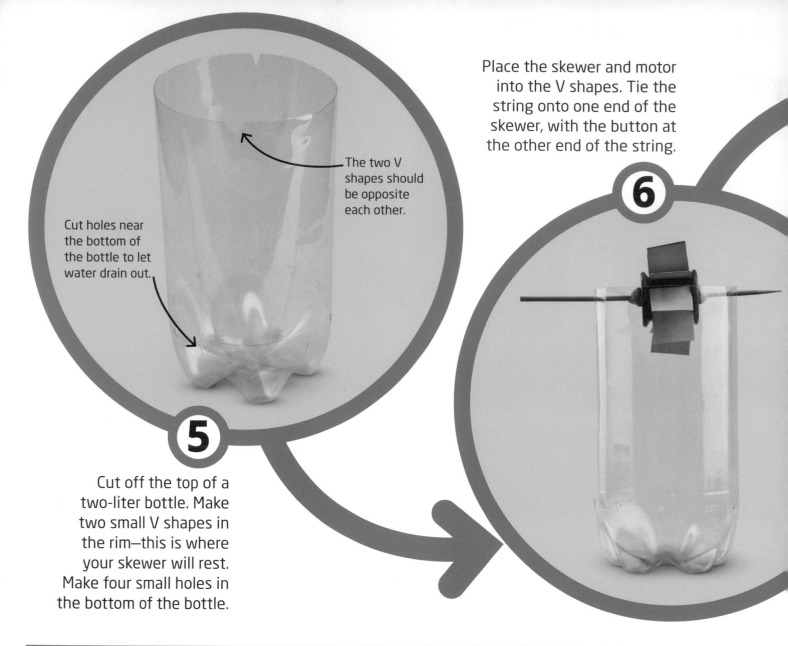

The two V shapes should be opposite each other.

Cut holes near the bottom of the bottle to let water drain out.

Place the skewer and motor into the V shapes. Tie the string onto one end of the skewer, with the button at the other end of the string.

6

5

Cut off the top of a two-liter bottle. Make two small V shapes in the rim—this is where your skewer will rest. Make four small holes in the bottom of the bottle.

Water power

Turbines use liquids, steam, or gas to spin their blades quickly enough to make electricity. When this process uses water, it is called hydroelectric power. Hydroelectric power plants are often built with dams that control the water flow, so they can create as much power as possible.

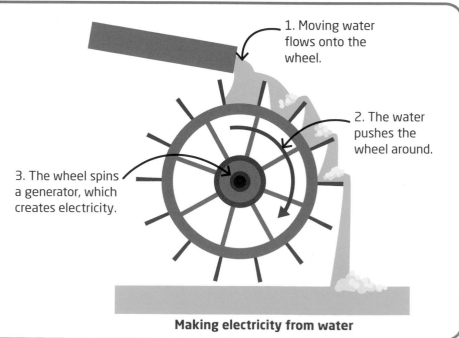

1. Moving water flows onto the wheel.

2. The water pushes the wheel around.

3. The wheel spins a generator, which creates electricity.

Making electricity from water

Tie one end of your string to the skewer and the other to the button.

As the motor spins, the string will wrap around the skewer, lifting the button up.

7 Place the whole structure under a faucet, and turn on the water. The running water should spin your motor around.

Did you know?

Engineers find out lots of cool facts as they investigate the world around them. How many of these facts do you know?

Types of engineering

Engineers are all around us, but they don't all do the same job. There are lots of different types of engineering—let's take a closer look.

 Electrical Electrical engineers build electrical systems, such as circuits, electrical grids, and signals.

 Mechanical Mechanical engineers design machines. Engines, cars, and roller coasters are created by mechanical engineers.

 Civil Civil engineers design and build bridges, tunnels, roads, and buildings. They help make things we couldn't live without.

 Industrial Industrial engineers make processes faster and easier—for example, by creating production lines in factories.

 Chemical Chemical engineers work in labs. They turn raw materials into medicine, food, and clothes.

 Bioengineering Bioengineers work with doctors and researchers to develop new technology, such as robotic limbs.

 Software Software engineers create code and programs that make computers work.

 Aerospace Aerospace engineers build machines that can fly, such as planes and spacecraft.

The fastest trains in the world

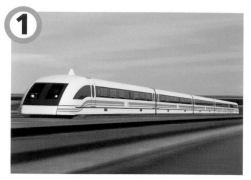

1

Shanghai Maglev The fastest train in the world is the Shanghai Maglev, from China. It can reach speeds of up to 267 mph (430 kph).

2

Harmony CRH380A China also holds the title for the second-fastest train. The Harmony CRH380A can travel as fast as 236 mph (380 kph). Up to 480 people can fit inside it.

3

AGV Italo In third place is the AGV Italo, from Italy. It travels up to 220 mph (360 kph) and connects most of Italy's big cities.

Wing shape

The shape of a plane's wings affect how it flies. Wings that bend downward are called anhedral wings. Wings that bend upward are called dihedral wings. These wing shapes are used for different types of planes.

Anhedral This type of wing is used for small, fast planes, such as fighter planes. The downward shape lets the plane spin and turn quickly.

Dihedral This type of wing is used for passenger planes. The upward shape of the wing allows the plane to fly straight for long distances.

Types of power

Solar Solar panels absorb light from the sun and turn it into electricity. They work best in sunny areas.

Fossil fuels Coal, gas, and oil are fossil fuels that can be burned to create energy. This type of power is non-renewable—one day the supply of fossil fuels will run out.

Wind Turbines turn in the wind. They change movement energy into electrical energy. This type of power is renewable, which means it will not run out.

Geothermal Below earth's surface, it is very hot. This heat can be used to turn water into steam, which moves a turbine, creating electricity.

Water Flowing water can be used to turn turbines inside a dam. The spinning turbines create electricity.

Nuclear Nuclear power uses fission—a process in which atoms are split apart, releasing huge amounts of energy. This produces steam that turns a turbine to create electricity.

Glossary

airfoil shape of the wing of an aircraft

aerospace engineering projects related to aircraft and spacecraft

architect person who plans and designs buildings

astronaut someone who is trained to travel and work in a spacecraft

atom smallest part of something that can take part in a chemical reaction

automatic something that works on its own without human help

bridge a structure carrying a road or path over a road, railroad, canyon, or body of water

buoyancy upward push that makes objects float on water

cable thick wire rope used in building

cantilever bridge that is only supported at one end

cargo objects that are carried by ship, plane, train, or other vehicle

chemical substance made by a reaction between particles such as atoms

chemical engineering science that uses chemicals to make new products

chemist someone who studies chemicals and their reactions

civil engineering designing projects such as bridges, buildings, and roads

composite something made from several parts or materials

compress flatten

computer machine that can perform difficult tasks by following instructions

computer programmer person who writes programs for computers

corrosion process where metals break down after contact with oxygen and water

data information

density how much of something there is in a certain amount of space. If two things take up the same amount of space, the denser one will have more in it and be heavier

design to plan and figure out how something will work and what it will look like

drag force that works to slow down an object as it travels through air or water

electricity flow of electric charge that powers things

energy source of power such as electrical energy or heat energy

engine machine that powers vehicles by burning fuel to release energy

engineer someone who uses science and math to solve technical problems

environment area that someone lives in, or that a machine works in

environmental engineering projects related to the world around us

experiment test to see how something works

flexible bendable

float ability to stay at the surface of a liquid

fluid substance, such as a gas or a liquid, that can flow easily and does not have a fixed shape

force push or pull that causes things to move, change direction, change speed, or stop moving

fossil fuels fuels made from animals and plants that died millions of years ago—for example, coal

friction force created when two surfaces rub or slide against each other

fuel substance that is burned to create heat or power

fulcrum point that a lever is supported on

galvanization process of covering a metal with a protective coating to keep it from rusting

gravity attraction between everything in the universe, which pulls objects toward Earth

hardware physical parts of a computer

hull main body of a ship

humanoid robot that looks and moves like a human

input devices that people use to tell a computer what to do—for example, a mouse or keyboard

invention new idea that solves a problem

machine something that is powered by energy and is used to carry out a task

manufactured made by humans rather than occurring naturally

masonry using bricks and mortar to create structures

material substance that is used to make or build things

mechanical something that is controlled by a machine

mechanical engineering engineering that designs and makes machines

mortar paste that glues building blocks together

nanotechnology science that deals with making very small technology

particle something that is very small, such as a proton or neutron

pollution harmful substances in the air, soil, or water

polymer chain of thousands of atoms

power source energy that is used to make a machine work, such as electricity

program set of instructions a computer follows to complete a task

renewable type of energy that can be produced without polluting the air or water, such as solar or wind power

robot machine that is programmed by a computer to do different tasks

rotor spinning blades on a helicopter that help it lift off into the air

rover vehicle that explores other planets

sink inability to stay at the surface of a liquid

skyscraper very tall building made from light but strong materials

software programs and instructions used by a computer

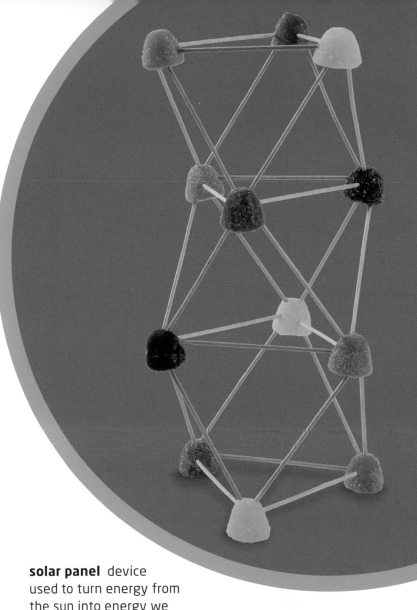

solar panel device used to turn energy from the sun into energy we can use

structure building that is made up of several parts

sustainable energy or materials that can keep going for a long time

synthetic something that is human made

taut tight

technology using scientific knowledge to create machinery and devices, such as computers

transfer when energy is moved from one place to another, or an object moves from one place to another

transportation moving people or goods by vehicle, such as ship, train, or plane

tunnel passage that goes underground

turbine wheel or rotor that is turned to make power

Index

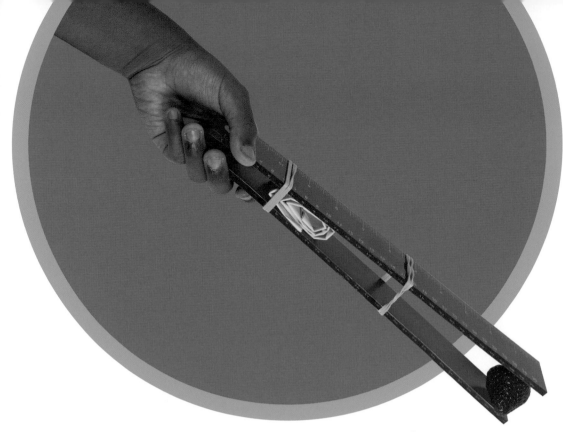

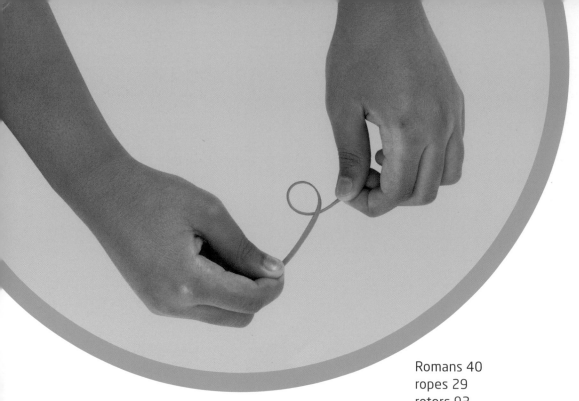

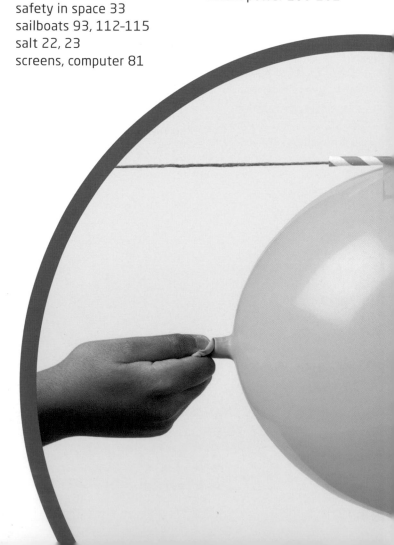

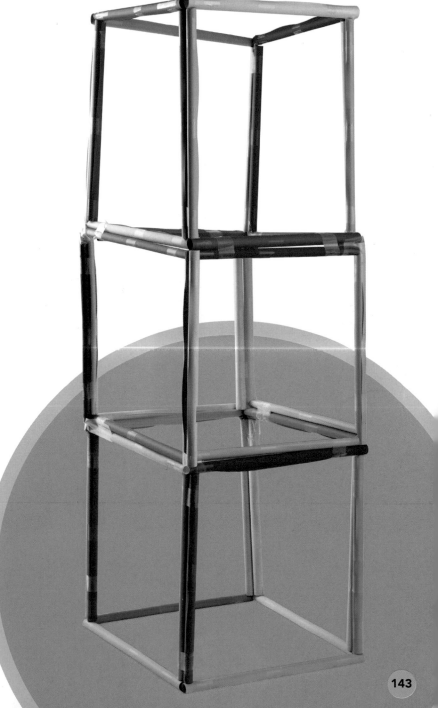

Acknowledgments

DK would like to thank the following: Katie Knutton for the illustrations; Caroline Hunt for proofreading; Helen Peters for the index; Richard Leeney for photography; Jo Clark, Alex Park, Maria Roinishvili, Claire Rugg, and Jack Whyte for modeling; Anne Damerell for legal assistance; and Nand Kishor Acharya, Yamini Panwar, and Pankaj Sharma for picture cutouts.

The publisher would like to thank the following for their kind permission to reproduce their photographs:

(Key: a-above; b-below/bottom; c-center; f-far; l-left; r-right; t-top)

4 Dorling Kindersley: Richard Leeney / RAF Boulmer, Northumberland (cra). **Humanoid robot created by Softbank Robotics:** (clb). **8 Dreamstime.com:** Wellphotos (br). **10-11 Dreamstime.com:** Dmitri Mihhailov. **12 Dreamstime.com:** Alfio Scisetti / Scisettialfio (cra). **13 123RF.com:** Mykola Davydenko / bestfotostudio (tr). **Dreamstime.com:** Eduard Bonnin Turina / Bonninturina (crb). **14 Dreamstime.com:** Wisconsinart (crb). **17 123RF.com:** alekss (cra). **22 123RF.com:** petkov (tc). **24 NASA:** (clb). **24-25 Alamy Stock Photo:** NG Images (c). **27 Getty Images:** Monty Rakusen (crb). **28 123RF.com:** Doug Cwiak (bc/Gloves); prakasitlalao (bl). **Dreamstime.com:** Goce Risteski / Goce (cb). **29 123RF.com:** Oleksii Sergieiev / sergieiev (tc); snak (bl); Gontar Valeriy (bl/Rope). **Alamy Stock Photo:** All Canada Photos (clb). **Dreamstime.com:** Kari Høglund / Karidesign (cra); Jose Manuel Gelpi Diaz (br). **33 NASA:** (crb). **34-35 Dreamstime.com:** Luckydoor. **37 Alamy Stock Photo:** robertharding (br). **38 Dreamstime.com:** Torsakarin (clb). **39 123RF.com:** Rolf Svedjeholm / rolf52 (tl). **Alamy Stock Photo:** Xinhua (tr). **Dreamstime.com:** lofoto (crb). **43 123RF.com:** Francesco Dazzi (cla). **44-45 123RF.com:** sergein. **45 Alamy Stock Photo:** Mike Goldwater (tr). **47 Getty Images:** Boris Horvat / Staff (cra). **49 Dreamstime.com:** Alexander Pladdet (crb). **50-51 Alamy Stock Photo:** Barry Bateman (bc). **51 Alamy Stock Photo:** Granger Historical Picture Archive (cl); Premier (tr). **58-59 Getty Images:** Heye Jensen / EyeEm. **60 123RF.com:** Stephen Gibson (bl). **Alamy Stock Photo:** Dave Gibbeson (cra). **61 123RF.com:** Olesia Bilkei (cra); Chris Dorney (cla). **iStockphoto.com:** stevecoleimages (br). **62 Dreamstime.com:** Shariff Che' Lah / Shariffc (tr). **64-65 Alamy Stock Photo:** World History Archive (c). **65 Alamy Stock Photo:** Dennis Hallinan (br). **73 123RF.com:** cherkas (tc). **75 Dreamstime.com:** Dikiiy (crb). **76-77 iStockphoto.com:** 3alexd (ca). **76 Humanoid robot created by Softbank Robotics:** (br). **NASA:** (bl). **77 123RF.com:** Mile Atanasov (clb); Aleksei Sysoev (tr). **Dreamstime.com:** Wellphotos (br). **78 Dorling Kindersley:** Clive Streeter / The Science

Museum, London (br). **80 123RF.com:** golubovy (br). **80-81 Dreamstime.com:** Orcea David / Orcearo (c). **81 123RF.com:** golubovy (bl, bc); PÃ © ter Gudella (br). **Dreamstime.com:** Ifeelstock (crb); Sergiy Mashchenko / Pulsar124 (cra). **82 Alamy Stock Photo:** john norman (clb). **83 Alamy Stock Photo:** Science History Images (tl, cr). **90-91 Getty Images:** Westend61. **92 Dreamstime.com:** Darkmonk (clb). **92-93 Dreamstime.com:** Ilfede (bc). **93 123RF.com:** Leonid Andronov (cra); Yury Gubin (crb). **Dorling Kindersley:** Richard Leeney / RAF Boulmer, Northumberland (tl). **98-99 Dorling Kindersley:** Gary Ombler / The National Railway Museum, York / Science Museum Group (br). **98 Alamy Stock Photo:** Chronicle (bl). **104 Alamy Stock Photo:** World History Archive (br). **104-105 Dorling Kindersley:** Flight (cr). **105 Alamy Stock Photo:** LOC Photo (tr). **Dreamstime.com:** Ekaterina Semenova / Ekaterinasemenova (br). **107 Dorling Kindersley:** Richard Leeney / Search and Rescue Hovercraft, Richmond, British Columbia (tr). **109 NASA:** (br). **116-117 Dreamstime.com:** Sergey Volkov. **118 123RF.com:** Artit Fongfung (cr). **Dreamstime.com:** Akulamatiau (bl). **118-119**

Dreamstime.com: Ivansmuk (tc). **119 Dorling Kindersley:** Stephen Oliver (bl). **122 Alamy Stock Photo:** Science History Images (bl). **122-123 Alamy Stock Photo:** Chronicle (c). **124 123RF.com:** cobalt (clb). **Dreamstime.com:** Manaemedia (bc); Anan Punyod (tr). **125 Dreamstime.com:** Broker (crb); Heike Falkenberg / Dslrpix (tl); Danicek (cra). **127 Getty Images:** Andia / Universal Images Group (cra). **131 Dreamstime.com:** Jjspring (cra). **132 Dorling Kindersley:** Ruth Jenkinson (tl). **136 Alamy Stock Photo:** Matthias Scholz (crb). **Dreamstime.com:** Beijing Hetuchuangyi Images Co, . Ltd . / Eastphoto (cra). **Getty Images:** VCG / Visual China Group (cr). **137 123RF.com:** jezper (clb); skylightpictures (bl). **Dreamstime.com:** Danicek (cr); Darren Baker / Darrenbaker (cl); Selitbul (crb). **Getty Images:** HIGH-G Productions / Stocktrek Images (tr); AFP / Staff (cra)

Cover images: *Front:* **Alamy Stock Photo:** David Kleyn bc

All other images © Dorling Kindersley For further information see: www.dkimages.com